100 Vedic Women

Shubha Vilas

Untold Tales From Indian Folklore

Om Books International

First published in 2024

Om Books International

Corporate & Editorial Office
A-12, Sector 64, Noida 201 301
Uttar Pradesh, India
Phone: +91 120 477 4100
Email: editorial@ombooks.com
Website: www.ombooksinternational.com

Sales Office
107, Ansari Road, Darya Ganj
New Delhi 110 002, India
Phone: +91 11 4000 9000
Email: sales@ombooks.com
Website: www.ombooks.com

© Om Books International 2024

Illustrated by: Shalini Soni Mazumdar

ALL RIGHTS RESERVED. No part of this book may be reproduced or transmitted in any form by any means, electronic or mechanical, including photocopying and recording, or by any information storage and retrieval system, except as may be expressly permitted in writing by the publisher.

ISBN: 978-81-95955-88-6

Printed in India

10 9 8 7 6 5 4 3 2 1

Contents

Aditi	9	Bhudevi	25
Andal	11	Chitrangada	27
Anjana	13	Damayanti	29
Anusuya	15	Devahuti	31
Apala	17	Devaki	33
Arundhati	19	Devayani	35
Bhangaswana	21	Devika, Vidura's Wife	37
Bhanumati	23	Diti	39

Draupadi	41
Durga	43
Dushala	45
Gandhari	47
Ganga	49
Gargi	51
Ghosha	53
Hemalekha	55
Hemapsara	57
Hidimbi	59
Indrani or Sachi	61
Indumati	63
Jahnava Devi	65
Jambavati	67
Kaikeyi	69
Kannagi	71
Kaushalya	73
Kaushaki	75
Kaveri	77
Kripi	79
Krishna and the Women	81
Kubja	83

Kunti		85	Mirabai	107
Lakshmana		87	Mitravinda	109
Lakshmi		89	Mohini Murti	111
Lankini		91	Narmada	113
Lopamudra		93	Parvati	115
Madalasa		95	Radha, Karna's Mother	117
Madhavi		97	Radharani	119
Madri		99	Rati - Wife of Kamadeva	121
Maitreyi		101	Revati	123
Mandavi		103	Rohini	125
Mandodari		105	Rukmini	127

Ruma		129	Shanta	151
Sachi Mata		131	Shikhandi	153
Sarama		133	Sita	155
Saranya		135	Subhadra	157
Saraswati		137	Sulochana	159
Sati		139	Sumitra	161
Satyabhama		141	Suniti	163
Satyavati		143	Surasa	165
Savitri		145	Susheela	167
Shabari		147	Swayamprabha	169
Shakuntala		149	Tara	171

The Wives of Kaliya		173	Uttara	191
Tilottama		175	Urvashi	193
Trijata		177	Vedavati	195
Tulasi		179	Vidula	197
Ubhaya Bharataai		181	Vinata	199
Ulupi		183	Vishnupriya	201
Uma Haimavati		185	Vrushali	203
Urmila		187	Yamuna	205
Usha		189	Yashoda	207

Aditi

From Srimad Bhagavatam

This is the story of Aditi who was among the thirteen daughters of Daksha, the divine king-rishi and son of Brahma. Aditi was a devoted daughter, beloved wife, and a benevolent mother. Aditi and her sister Diti were married to Sage Kashyapa. All the living entities owe their existence to them. All the devatas are known as 'Aditeyas' because they are the children of Aditi. It is mentioned in the Ramayana and the Mahabharata that Aditi was so fond of Lord Vishnu that she wanted to be his mother. Vishnu respected Aditi so much that he agreed to be born as her son. That is how Mahavishnu was born to Aditi as Vamana Dev.

Aditi was the mother of Indra, the king of gods. Once, Indra presented his mother a pair of earrings, which he had received as a gift for churning the ocean. But they were no ordinary earrings. The earrings had the special power to enhance the senses of the wearer which kept them away from danger. Aditi was delighted to receive such a precious gift from her son.

When the demon Narakasura heard about the powerful earrings, he attacked heaven and stole the earrings from Aditi. Indra tried his best, but could not stop the powerful demon. Alas, he had to ask for Krishna's help. Krishna, who loved his own mother dearly, heard that Narakasura had assaulted Indra's mother, Aditi, and decided to help him.

Krishna bravely fought Narakasura and killed the demon's entire army. Narakasura also fell dead in the battle. Krishna released all the 16,000 princesses whom Narakasura had kidnapped and locked in his palace. He also found Aditi's precious earrings and returned them to her. Aditi was joyful to have her earrings back.

Andal

From Srivilliputhur Sthala Purana

Vishnucitta was a devout follower of Lord Vishnu. One day, while plucking flowers from the temple garden for Lord Vishnu's worship, he found a little baby under a tulasi plant. He believed the little baby to be a gift from God. He decided to name the baby 'Godai', meaning 'gift of Mother Earth'. Vishnucitta raised Godai with extreme love and care. He sang songs to her about Krishna and shared with her his love of poetry and philosophy.

As Godai grew up, she inherited her father's love for Krishna. Her love grew so intense that she decided to marry only Krishna. She would sing songs of his glories and dream about marrying her beloved Krishna one day.

However, Godai's passion started to worry Vishnucitta. One night, he had a dream where Lord Ranganatha assured him that he would marry Godai, and so he should start preparing for the wedding. And that is how Godai came to be known as Andal, which means 'the one who ruled God'.

The next day, Andal was prepared to marry her love and dressed herself in the finest bridal attire. She was taken in a palanquin to Ranganatha's temple. Upon reaching the temple, the 15-year-old girl jumped out of the palanquin in excitement and ran inside the sanctum. As soon as Andal hugged Ranganatha's idol, she disappeared in a blaze, uniting with it. Andal finally got to marry her Lord, and the united deity came to be known as Rangamannar.

Andal was the only woman among the twelve Alvar poet-saints of South India. She was believed to be the human incarnation of the goddess Bhumi Devi, the consort of Lord Narayana. Andal led a remarkable life. She is remembered for her love and devotion.

Anjana
From Ramayana

Thousands of years ago, lived a Vanara woman named Anjana. Anjana was a great tapasvi. She performed great austerities seated in a cave on a mountain. One day, she was attacked by a demon named Shambhasadhana. To save herself from him, she sprinted, jumped and swung from branches to reach the ashram of a sage. The sage informed her that only Kesari, the monkey-king, had the capability to stand up to the demon.

Kesari surprisingly appeared as soon as his name was uttered. He took it upon himself to save the situation and protect Anjana and the sages from the evil demon. The shape-changing demon fought tooth and nail but Kesari was a tough match. When the fight seemed to reach a deadlock, Anjana went into meditation to find an answer to help Kesari.

While meditating, an unknown voice suggested that the demon could be killed only with his own blood. She took Kesari's arrow and after dipping it in the demon's blood, returned it to Kesari. As Kesari shot the arrow given by Anjana, the demon fell to the ground and died. The sages blessed Kesari and Anjana to get married and predicted that the child born to them would be the saviour of the world. After a while, Anjana decided to purify herself to conceive a child. When she was in intense meditation, the god of wind dropped Shiva's conception into her palms. This is how Hanuman, Shiva's incarnation, was born.

Anjana raised Hanuman to be an ardent devotee of Shri Rama. Anjana, an exceptional woman, gave birth to a noble son.

Anusuya
From Ramayana

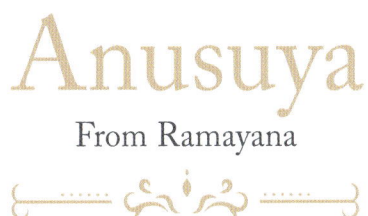

Anusuya was a woman with mystical powers obtained from her strict practice of austerities. Once, goddesses Parvati, Lakshmi and Saraswati persuaded their husbands, the holy Trinity, to go and test her. Disguised as illustrious sages, they went to Anusuya and made a bizarre request – to feed them without clothes. Anusuya was surprised, but used her wisdom. Chanting some mantras, she sprinkled holy water on the disguised gods who instantly turned into innocent toddlers. Then, Anusuya shed her clothes and fed them. She felt motherly love towards them and decided not to turn them into adults again.

The three goddesses were worried when their husbands did not return. They reached Anusuya's abode in search of them. Seeing the three goddesses together, Anusuya respectfully sought their blessings. When they revealed the truth, Anusuya quickly chanted some mantras and the toddlers became Brahma, Vishnu and Mahesh who offered her a boon. Anusuya and her husband Saptarshi Atri asked for three children. The gods gladly consented. The first child Chandra was the incarnation of Lord Brahma, the second child Durvasa was the incarnation of Lord Shiva and the third one Dattatreya was an incarnation of Lord Vishnu.

Apala
From Rigveda

Sage Atri's daughter Apala is mentioned in the Rigveda as a *brahmavadini*. Apala had an incurable skin disease which made her life very difficult and she was abandoned by her husband. Saddened and troubled by her condition, she asked her father for advice. Atri advised her to do extreme penance and please Lord Indra. Apala took her father's advice seriously and did severe penance for a very long time. When finally Indra appeared in front of her, she offered him the juice of a somlata plant. This pleased Indra greatly. Apala then asked him for three boons.

She firstly hoped to make her father's barren field fertile. Next, she wished for her bald father to have hair on his head. And last, she wished for a miracle cure to treat her skin disease. Indra did not hesitate to fulfil her wishes. After granting the first two wishes, Indra gave her triple cleansing. He cleansed her human body first, then her vital force, and finally her soul. After thorough cleansing, Apala's disease vanished, and she transformed into a beautiful damsel.

Arundhati

From Ramayana

Arundhati is one of the most revered and inspirational women of Vedic times. She was the wife of Sage Vashishtha, one of the Saptarshis. Her scholarly status is considered being on par with the rishis. Many Vedic rituals are centred on Arundhati, including the Saptapadi ritual in a marriage ceremony.

Arundhati was the daughter of Kardama Muni and Devahuti. She was Sage Parashara's grandmother and Sage Vyasa's great-grandmother. Arundhati had one hundred sons, but they were all killed by Sage Vishwamitra. She had eight more sons after that. Two of her sons - Shakti and Suyagya - received their education along with Rama in Sage Vashishtha's hermitage.

Arundhati was also the mentor of the Raghu clan and the guardian angel of Sita. When Rama banished Sita, there was a huge uproar. Sita's father Janak strongly condemned this act. Arundhati played the role of a peacemaker by using empathy and other tactics to resolve the conflict between Rama and Janaka.

Once, Swaha, wife of Agni had taken the guise of Saptarshis' wives. However, she could not assume the form of the pure Arundhati. Arundhati was the personification of devotion, wisdom and purity.

Bhangaswana

From Ramayana

King Bhangaswana had once offended the mighty Indra. Indra waited for an opportunity to seek revenge.

One day on a hunting expedition, Bhangaswana lost his way. Wandering alone, he stumbled upon a lake. He waded inside and quenched his parched throat. When he emerged out of the water, he was shocked to see that he had transformed into a woman. Bhangaswana then left his kingdom to his hundred sons and left. Soon he married a tribal man. He mothered another hundred sons and sent them all to his kingdom. Now there were 200 powerful sons of the king at the helm.

Indra decided to stir up the king's life again. He sowed the seeds of jealousy among the two groups of brothers who went to war and killed each other. The king was in agony at the loss of his 200 sons.

Indra now wanted to repent for his deeds. He told the king that he would restore half of his sons back to life. The king, in her female form, replied with folded hands, "I want all the sons I have mothered back to life."

Indra asked, "Why?" She replied, "The love and affection a mother has for her sons is far greater than the love a father has for his sons."

Indra restored all the 200 sons back to life. He even proposed to restore his original glory of a powerful king. But the female form of the king replied, "I wish to remain a woman. The pleasure of motherhood far surpasses that of fatherhood. The joy I get in seeing my sons was never mine as a father. I don't wish to lose that joy. Please let me remain a mother for the entire world."

Indra left from there with new insights and lessons.

Bhanumati

From Shanti Parva, Mahabharata

Bhanumati, a young and dynamic damsel, was the daughter of Chitrangada, the King of Kalinga. The king held a swayamvar for his precious daughter and invited all the suitable princes from far and wide. Among the suitors were Duryodhana, Shishupala, Jarasandha and Bhishmaka. All of them were eager to win the hand of the fair maiden.

The stunning Bhanumati, surrounded by her bodyguards, arrived in the hall holding a garland. As soon as Duryodhana saw her, he fell in love. Bhanumati's friend announced the lineage and qualities of each prince whom she met. When she reached Duryodhana, Bhanumati heard about him but moved ahead. Pained by this rejection and humiliation, in a flash, Duryodhana grabbed her and fled in his chariot.

Once the remaining guests realised what had happened, they felt insulted and chased Duryodhana to rescue Bhanumati and win her heart. Duryodhana's best friend, Karna, however, held back the princes, allowing Duryodhana to flee. Bhanumati was not sure about marrying Duryodhana but agreed when he cited Bhishma's example who had kidnapped three sisters to marry his stepbrother. They had a son, Laxman, and a daughter, Laxmana. Laxman died in the Mahabharata war and Laxmana was married to Samba, Krishna's son.

Bhanumati was a strong-willed woman who never hesitated to speak her mind. It is believed that she tried to stop Duryodhana from disrobing Draupadi, as she feared that the backlash would be destructive for the Kurus.

Bhudevi

From Srimad Bhagavatam, Ramayana

Bhudevi, also known as Bhumidevi, is the goddess representing the Earth. She is the mate of Varaha Deva, the third avatar of Lord Vishnu.

In Satya Yuga, Bhudevi was kidnapped by an arrogant demon called Hiranyaksha and hidden deep in the cosmic ocean. Lord Vishnu appeared as Varah Deva to save the distressed goddess from the notorious demon. After slaying the demon, he lifted Bhumidevi on his tusks and placed her back to her place in the Universe. Soon after, the two got married.

In Treta Yuga, Rama's wife Sita was known as the daughter of Bhumi because King Janaka found her while ploughing land in Mithila. Janaka and his wife adopted her but considered her to be the daughter of the Earth. Thus, Sita was called Bhumija.

Bhudevi and Varah Deva had a son together, called Narakasura. Narakasura did immense penance to get a boon. He asked that he would not be killed by anyone but his own mother. He believed that his mother would never kill him, which practically made him immortal. This made him feel powerful and undefeatable. Drunk with power, he kidnapped 16,000 women and made them his wives. He waged war on heaven and even stole Indra's mother's mystical earrings. Finally, the gods asked Bhudevi to kill her son. She appeared as Satyabhama, Krishna's wife in Dvapara Yuga and, with his help, killed Narakasura.

Bhudevi has the ability to withstand any problems that occur on Earth. We pray to her for patience, knowledge, wisdom, wealth, courage and boldness in our lives.

Chitrangada
From Mahabharata

Chitrangada was the daughter of King Chitravahana of Manipur. She was an extremely agile warrior and the only heir to her father's throne. Once, during his travels, Arjuna reached Manipur, where he saw the beautiful warrior princess. He fell in love with her instantly and asked her father for her hand in marriage.

King Chitravahana told Arjuna the story of their ancestor, King Prabhanjana, who was childless and took up austerities to please Lord Shiva. Being pleased with Prabhanjana's sincerity, Lord Shiva offered him the boon that all his future descendants would each have just one child. Accordingly, each person in his dynasty had one son, but Chitravahana had a daughter. Instead of fretting, he trained his daughter in warfare and taught her the skills to carry out the responsibilities of the kingdom. He put forth the condition that the son born out of the marriage between Arjuna and Chitrangada would be Chitravahana's successor to the royal throne.

Arjuna agreed to the king's condition and married Chitrangada. They lived together for three years. When Chitrangada gave birth to a son named Babruvahan, Arjuna left to resume his journey. Chitrangada stayed back to raise her son and take care of her father's kingdom.

Damayanti
From Mahabharata

Born to King Bhishma of Vidarbha, Damayanti was an enchanting woman who was desired even by the gods. However, Damayanti fell in love with Nala, the ruler of the Nishada kingdom, after the king sent a swan to tell her about him. Her father had organised a Swayamvara for her and invited the most capable men. As Nala was on his way to the Swayamvara, he was intimidated by four demigods to convey the message that Damayanti must choose one of the four gods as her husband, and not Nala. Damayanti, although confused by the message, kept faith in Nala's love for her. Upon reaching the Swayamvara with a garland in her hand, she was shocked to see five Nalas standing in front of her. She realised it was a test by the gods. Damayanti, with her love and faith, found the real Nala. With profuse blessings of the four gods, Nala and Damayanti got married.

There was someone who was jealous of their happiness. Kali, the personification of Kali Yuga, had also wanted to marry Damayanti and got angry upon learning that Damayanti chose a mortal over the gods. He decided to ruin Nala's life and waited for twelve years to find a weakness and enter Nala's body. Kali destroyed Nala's mind due to which Nala lost his kingdom in a game with his brother, Pushkara. He had to go into exile in a forest with Damayanti. One night in the forest, stricken with grief and embarrassment, Nala abandoned Damayanti. With great difficulties, Damayanti reached her parents' home. But Damayanti never gave up hope and with her unbreakable trust, managed to return to Nala. Soon Nala won back his kingdom and the two lived a long and happy life together.

Devahuti

From Srimad Bhagavatam

Devahuti was the daughter of Svayambhuva Manu. She was the wife of Kardama Muni. Devahuti was a beautiful and learned woman who believed that spiritual knowledge and peace were greater than any worldly pleasures. She chose to marry an ascetic because of her ideals and the desire to lead a spiritual life.

Born from the shadow of Brahma, Kardama Muni lived on the banks of the Bindu Sarovar. He was approached by Svayambhuva Manu with Devahuti's hand in marriage. Kardama Muni had been blessed by Lord Vishnu to have a pure and beautiful wife who would give birth to nine daughters and one son. The nine daughters would eventually give birth to great sages and the son would be the Supreme Lord incarnated. Kardama Muni agreed to marry Devahuti on the condition that after the birth of a son, he would leave for the forest to remain in seclusion for the rest of his life. The two married and lived happily for many years. Nine beautiful daughters were born to Devahuti who got married to nine prajapatis created by Brahma. Eventually, a son was born to the couple. They named him Kapila. As soon as Kapila was born, Kardama Muni left for the forest for meditation and penance. Devahuti raised the child herself. Kapila grew up to be an esteemed sage and the founder of the Sankhya philosophy.

Devahuti approached his son to instruct her on the path of bhaktiyog. Delighted by her son's knowledge, Devahuti perfected her life and became a brahmavadini. She could achieve peace of mind and became one with God.

Devaki

From Srimad Bhagavatam

Devaki was born to King Devak and married to Vasudeva. She was the cousin sister of Kamsa, who imprisoned his own father and took over the throne of Mathura. Kamsa was a cruel tyrant, but he loved Devaki dearly.

After the marriage ceremony of Devaki and Vasudeva, Kamsa chose to drive the couple's chariot. Suddenly, a celestial voice declared that the eighth child of Devaki would cause Kamsa's death. Angered and panicked by the prophecy, Kamsa decided to kill Devaki. Vasudeva, in his attempt to save Devaki's life, promised to give each of their children to Kamsa, whom he could kill. Kamsa agreed and put the newlywed couple in jail. From then on, Kamsa would mercilessly kill each child born to Vasudeva and Devaki. When the eighth child was born, he appeared in his divine form with four fully decorated hands, holding weapons and a head full of hair. Devaki requested him to hide his original form and appear as an ordinary child. She was scared that Kamsa would harm him if he found that the Supreme Lord had appeared. Seeing her motherly love, the god obliged. Soon after, Vasudeva secretly carried the little Krishna across the Yamuna and exchanged him with Yashoda's daughter.

Devaki spent several years in prison, away from her beloved son. She waited patiently for her son to rescue her so that she could be reunited with him. Devaki was a devout wife and a loving mother who had to bear witness to the loss of her children repeatedly. Eventually, she got to see and feed her dead sons with the help and blessing of Krishna.

Devayani
From Srimad Bhagavatam

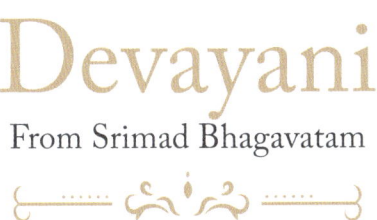

Devayani was the daughter of the guru of the asuras, Shukracharya, and his wife Jayanti, the daughter of Indra. Being born to such a powerful sage like Shukracharya, she would often meet people in powerful positions.

Devayani befriended Sharmishtha, the daughter of King Vrisparva, to whom Shukracharya was an advisor. The two girls became good friends who would do everything together. One day, Sharmishtha and Devayani went for a bath in a river in the forest with Sharmishtha's entourage. They laughed and chatted the whole day. After the bath, the mood suddenly shifted when Devayani wore Sharmishtha's sari by mistake. Even though the mistake on Devayani's part was innocent, Sharmishtha hurled insults at Devayani and reminded her of her status. In her anger, Sharmishtha ripped the sari off Devayani, pushed the unclad girl inside a dry well with the help of her friends, and left.

Scared of the consequences awaiting her, ashamed of her unclothed state and angry at the insult, Devayani shouted out for help. To her luck, King Yayati was passing by and heard the poor girl's cry for help. He helped her climb out of the well. Devayani returned to her father and narrated the entire incident to him. Rightly enraged, Shukracharya threatened Sharmishtha's father. When the king begged forgiveness, Shukracharya said that he would forgive him only if his daughter got what she wanted. Devayani, as revenge, asked to have Sharmishtha as her servant along with other asura girls. Eventually, Yayati and Devayani got married and had two sons.

Devika, Vidura's Wife
From Mahabharata

Dhritarashtra's half-brother Vidura was a great devotee of Krishna. His wife, Devika, was just as much smitten with Krishna. When Krishna visited the Kauravas in Hastinapur, he decided to eat at Vidura's house, rejecting the feast offered to him by Duryodhana. He even told Duryodhana that he ate only when someone fed him with love.

Devika, in her sublime bliss, waited eagerly for Krishna's arrival. She cleaned every corner of the house and cooked all kinds of delicious meals. As soon as she heard Krishna at the door, she rushed to welcome him. Upon seeing Krishna, she forgot about everything. She offered him bananas and peeled them herself. In a trance, she threw away the pulp and fed him the peels. She was so engrossed in her love that she barely realised what she was doing. Krishna was just as happy to witness her love and ate the banana peels with great joy.

When Vidura returned, he saw his wife feeding banana peels to Krishna, and chastised her. He offered the pulp to Krishna, but Krishna cheekily said that the peels from Devika's hand were much tastier.

Diti

From Srimad Bhagavatam

Diti belonged to an illustrious lineage with Daksha Prajapati as her father and Kasyapa, the grandson of Brahma, as her husband. While Diti was the mother of demons, her sister Aditi was the mother of devatas.

Demons and devatas were always at war with each other. There was one instance when they all got together. They joined forces to churn the ocean to extract the elixir from its depth. The venture, however, ended with the death of all of Diti's sons, the demons.

Inconsolable, Diti prayed to her husband for a heroic son who could avenge the death of his brothers. She wished for a braveheart who could slay Indra. Kashyapa blessed her with the boon that if she worshipped the Lord with a pure heart and mind for a hundred years, her wish would be fulfilled.

Diti embarked on this tiresome journey of devotion. Her sincerity and purity bore the result, and she soon became pregnant. When Indra heard the news, he was alarmed. In order to protect himself, he went to Diti disguised as her attendant to serve her during pregnancy. One night, after Diti went to bed, Indra ripped open her womb with his Vajra and cut the embryo inside it into seven pieces. When the embryo cried, Indra said, "Don't cry (Ma Ruda)". He cut each of the seven pieces further into seven pieces until there were forty-nine pieces. In this way, Diti gave birth to the "Maruts" who became devas and helped Indra in his endeavours.

Draupadi
Mahabharata

Born from a sacrificial fire, Draupadi was the daughter of King Drupada. Her life was just as extraordinary as her birth. Draupadi was the central character in the story of Mahabharata. She was not just beautiful, but also strong-willed and courageous. Her father arranged a Swayamvara to make sure that she married the most powerful man. He arranged the Swayamvara that only Arjuna could win. Arjuna performed the almost impossible task and won Draupadi's hand in marriage.

At that time, the Pandavas were living in hiding. Arjuna brought Draupadi home and told his mother Kunti that he had won a prize. Kunti was praying at the time, and without looking up, told Arjuna to share the prize with his brothers. Eventually, Draupadi got married to all five of them and became their uniting force.

When Yudhisthira conducted a Rajyasuya sacrifice that declared him the supreme king of the land and Draupadi the queen, Duryodhana got extremely spiteful. His envy resulted in the gambling match where the Pandavas lost everything, including Draupadi. Draupadi was publicly disrobed and humiliated by Duryodhana's brother, Duhshahsana. The Pandavas and Draupadi spent 13 years in exile and eventually returned with an enormous army of supporters to regain power over their kingdom. The war led to the destruction of all the Kauravas and thus, Draupadi's insult was avenged. Draupadi's insult.

Durga
From Devi Bhagavat

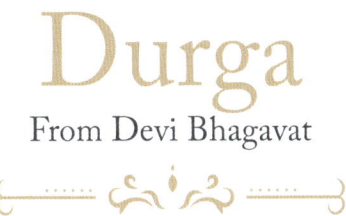

Durga has many names and forms. She is one of the most powerful goddesses in Hindu scriptures. As Kali, she turns black at night in rage and fury, with just a string of skulls as her garland. As Parvati, she is the calm and beautiful wife of Lord Shiva. She is the destroyer of evil.

Mahishasura was an extremely powerful demon. He dreamt of being the king of all worlds, but every time he went to war, he lost. He decided to perform austerities and gain mystical powers. He stood on one foot under a tree for many years. Finally, a pleased Brahma appeared before him. Mahishasura asked for the boon that he should not be not be killed by any man or god.

After receiving the boon, Mahishasura attacked Earth and Heaven. Vishnu, Brahma and Shiva attempted to save Heaven, but even their combined forces could not defeat the demon. Vishnu, Brahma and Shiva combined their energies again and focused intensely on creating an invincible woman. With the mix of their energies, a ball of fire appeared.

Shiva gave the mass of energy a face; Vishnu moulded her arms while Brahma shaped her legs. They armed her with the chakra, trident, and ganga water. Himalaya, the god of mountains, presented her with a mighty tiger to ride on. She was named Durga and with their blessings; she set out on her mission to end the demon's tyranny. The battle raged for nine days. Durga beheaded the demon and won the battle. Since then, Durga is worshipped for nine days and we celebrate these days as Navaratri.

Dushala

From Mahabharata

Gandhari, the queen of Hastinapur, had a hundred sons known as the Kauravas and one daughter, called Dushala. Growing up under the guidance of her grandfather Bhishma and with the love of her one hundred and five brothers, the Kauravas and the Pandavas, Dushala had a lovely childhood. However, her married life was not fulfilling. Her husband, Jayadratha, was the king of Sindhu. Jayadratha was an egoistic and evil king. He once tried to abduct Draupadi. The Pandavas prevented him from kidnapping Draupadi and were ready to slay him. Dushala intervened and begged for her husband's life. Upon their beloved cousin's request, the Pandavas spared Jayadratha's life.

Jayadratha had a boon from Shiva and using that boon, he killed Arjuna's son Abhimanyu mercilessly in the Mahabharata war. Incensed with Jayadratha, Arjuna killed him for revenge. Dushala became a widow and her son Suratha was crowned king of Sindhu. Not long after, Arjuna and his army came to Sindhu, following their horse for the Ashwamedha sacrifice. Suratha was killed by Arjuna in the battle. Dushala, who had already lost her husband, was shattered by the loss of her son. She carried her grandson in her arms and went to Arjuna, crying for mercy. Arjuna felt bad for his cousin and left Sindhu, crowning Dushala's grandson as the king.

Dushala, a pure and innocent woman who was loved by everyone, ultimately suffered a lot because of her husband's deeds and his enmity with the Pandavas.

Gandhari

From Mahabharata

Gandhari was the daughter of King Subala of Gandhar. She had a brother named Shakuni who loved her dearly. When Draupadi was young, she performed great tapasya to please Lord Shiva, who blessed her with the boon to have a hundred sons. Bhishma, upon learning of the boon, considered Gandhari to be an ideal match for Dhritarashtra, who was blind from birth. Gandhari showed her devotion to her husband by tying a cloth around her eyes. Soon after their marriage, Gandhari became pregnant, but the embryo remained in her womb for two years.

Meanwhile, her sister-in-law Kunti gave birth first and her son became the heir to the throne of Hastinapur. In frustration, Gandhari continuously hit her womb in sheer anger and envy, asking the child to come out. To her surprise, a lump of flesh fell off her womb. Vyasdeva was called to deal with the strange turn of events. He divided the lump into a hundred parts and put them in separate pots from which the Kauravas were born. Gandhari also had a daughter named Dushala. The Kauravas were unrighteous and cunning. Despite Gandhari's several requests to follow dharma, they refused to heed her advice. As a mother, she had no option but to support her sons. She even removed her blind-fold once to transfer all her power of tapasya and make Duryodhana's body strong as iron.

After the war, when Yudhishthira came to meet Gandhari, she could see his toe nail from the side of her blind-fold. She was so enraged that just by her fiery glance, his toe nail was charred. She even cursed Krishna that he would lose his entire dynasty because he did not intervene to prevent the war and save her sons from death.

Ganga
From Mahabharata

Bali, the king of demons, was growing in power, which gravely concerned Indra. So, Vishnu appeared in his Vamana avatar, a dwarf Brahmin, to help Indra retain his throne. Vamana asked Bali for three steps of land. Since he was a dwarf, Bali happily agreed to fulfil the Brahmin's wish against the desire of his guru, Shukracharya.

As soon as Bali agreed, Vamana expanded in size magically to become a giant. With one step, he covered the entire Earth! With his second step, he covered the skies. When the mighty God's foot was in the sky, Brahma washed it and collected the water in his kamandala. This holy water came to be known as Ganga.

Brahma released the holy water on Earth at the request of King Bhagiratha, who wished to atone for the sins of his ancestors. Ganga's power and fury was such that if she descended on Earth, she could sweep away everything. So, Shiva was requested to break Ganga's fall by catching her in his matted locks and gently releasing her again. This is how Ganga arrived on Earth as Bhagirathi. One time, she playfully flooded Sage Jahnu's ashram. The angry sage gobbled up all her water. Bhagiratha had to intervene again and request the sage to release her. The sage obliged and Ganga flowed out from his ears and came to be known as Jahnavi.

Ganga is regarded as the goddess of purification and forgiveness. She rides a makar—half crocodile and half fish with her streams traversing the heavens, hell, and Earth. In Mahabharata, Ganga was the first wife of the Kuru king Shantanu and the mother of Bhishma.

Gargi
From Ramayana

Gargi was born to Sage Vachaknu in the lineage of the renowned Sage Garga. From a young age, she showed a deep interest in the Vedic scriptures and spent all her time and effort to gain as much knowledge as she could. Because of her rigorous study, she was widely acclaimed as a scholar. She would often hold philosophical discussions with learned and competent scholars.

King Janaka, a patron of Vedic learning and scholarship, once conducted a Rajasuya Yagya and invited all the kings, princes and learned scholars to take part in the yagya. The yagya lasted for days with lively discussions and debates between the scholars. The king announced the prize of one thousand cows with 10 grams of gold dangling from their horns for the winner of the discussions. Among the scholars was the renowned sage Yajnavalkya, who had also mastered the art of Kundalini yoga. Most scholars did not dare to contest with him. He was so sure of his spiritual superiority over the others that he ordered his disciple to take the cows to his house. Eight renowned sages challenged him. Gargi was one of those sages and the only woman in the gathering.

The dialogue between Yajnavalkya and Gargi is eternally famous, highlighting the stature of Gargi. She had a deep inquisitiveness to unravel the mystery of the super soul, the nature of the individual soul, Brahman and the relationship between them. Gargi was even honoured as one of the Navaratnas (nine gems) in King Janaka's court. She is a pioneer of women's education and social equality.

Ghosha
From Rigveda

Ghosha is one of the famous female philosophers and seers of Vedic India. She is a Rishika who was highly knowledgeable and proficient in the Vedas. Her father Kakshivat and grandfather Dirghatamas had both composed hymns in the glory of Ashwins, the heavenly twin gods associated with medicine and health. Following their footsteps, Ghosha too composed two hymns of the Rig Veda, each containing 14 verses praising the Ashwins. Ghosha suffered from an incurable skin disease from childhood which had disfigured her. While her first hymn praised the Ashwins, her second hymn expressed her intimate desire for marriage and companionship.

In her growing years, she served her father dutifully and prayed continuously to the Ashwins to heal her disease and rejuvenate her. Her devotion pleased the brothers so much that they descended to teach her Madhu Vidya, which had the power to grant youth and health. The secret knowledge of Madhu Vidya cured her ailments and fulfilled her desire to get married.

She had a son named Suhastya who also composed hymns in the Rig Veda. Ghosha, a Brahmavadini, self-realised revealer of the Brahman, led a highly spiritual life and is cherished in the annals of Vedic history as a famous woman seer.

Hemalekha

From Tripura Rahasya

Hemalekha was the beautiful, adopted daughter of a sage. She was extremely learned and self-realised, happy in her blissful existence. However, this changed the day a prince stepped into their hermitage. The minute Prince Hemachuda glanced at Hemalekha, he fell helplessly in love with her. The sage saw the prince's obvious love for his daughter and agreed to the marriage.

The couple were wedded with great pomp. Several weeks went by in marital bliss till the prince noticed that his wife was not as passionate as he was in their relationship. Upon asking her the reason, the sagely Hemalekha answered him truthfully.

Hemalekha said that her spiritual upbringing had taught her that worldly objects were temporary and failed to give long-lasting pleasures. She searched for eternal pleasures. She had observed that the prince's father had unlimited wealth, yet he was never happy. Hemalekha believed that she could never seek pleasure in physical relationships connected to the body because it was the mind which concocted these pleasures.

Hemachuda was shaken up by his wife's answer. He was so affected that he could no longer enjoy the luxuries of his life. Hemalekha realised that her husband could be led on a spiritual path with the right guidance. She urged him to practise meditation and find his inner self which alone would bring him supreme joy.

Hemachuda followed her advice and soon found himself in a blissful condition where he was unaffected by any external factors. He had attained a yogic state. Not only he, but his parents, ministers and others also followed the spiritual path as shown by Hemalekha

Hemapsara
From Ramayana

Hema was a beautiful apsara in Indralok. On the day of her dance debut, she met her husband Mayasura, the asura king, and fell hopelessly in love with him. The asura king was equally in love with the extraordinary apsara.

Mayasura was blessed by Brahma to become the unrivalled architect amongst the devas and the asuras. His skills were unparalleled and even his enemies wanted to see the palaces he made. He proposed to Hema, and she gladly accepted. She trusted him with her whole heart. As Mayasura placed his hands on her eyes, closing them, she felt that she was floating in air. When she opened her eyes, they were standing in a spectacular city created by Mayasura. Mayasura added to her delight by telling her that this city shall be called Hemapura.

The couple spent many years in the city raising their two sons, Dundubhi and Mayavi. Hema yearned for a daughter and after great penance by Mayasura, Lord Shiva blessed them with a daughter. One day, a Brahmin came and gave them a girl child asking them to take care of her. The girl named Mandodari was an abode of divine qualities. Mandodari went on to become the demon Ravana's wife.

After many years of marital bliss, Hema's world came crashing down when Indra killed Mayasura. Her sons died at the hands of Vali, the vanara king. Unable to live in Hemapura without the love of her husband and children, Hema went back to Indralok.

Hidimbi

From Mahabharata

After the Pandavas escaped from their near-death experience in the palace of Lac, they helplessly roamed in a forest. They travelled inside the forest during daytime and halted at night in temporary makeshift places which Bhima would build.

One night, after the Pandavas and Kunti fell asleep, Bhima stood to guard his family. In the forest lived a man-eating demon called Hidimba, who smelt human flesh. After seeing a well-built man who would make a delicious meal, Hidimba sent his sister Hidimbi to lure the man. Hidimbi turned herself into a beautiful woman and as she approached Bhima, she lost her heart to him. She expressed her desire to marry him and even revealed her brother's intention to eat him. She showed Bhima her true form to express her earnest intentions. Hidimba found his sister talking to the human meal and felt enraged. Soon, a fight took place between Bhima and Hidimba. Bhima killed the demon with his powerful blows.

With Kunti's blessings, Hidimbi and Bhima got married. However, Kunti asked Hidimbi to allow Bhima to leave her after the birth of their child. Bhima put the condition that he shall spend the day with Hidimbi but, upon nightfall, return to the Pandavas and Kunti to guard them. Hidimbi agreed to the conditions and the two were married. Within a year, Hidimbi gave birth to a half-demon son who was named Ghatotkacha because his head looked like a pot. Soon, it was time for the couple to part ways. However, Bhima continued to visit Hidimbi and their son. This boy grew up to be a very courageous, mystical and powerful warrior who played a very crucial role in the Mahabharata war.

Indrani or Sachi

From Srimad Bhagavatam

Sachi Devi, also known as Indrani, is the queen of gods and the wife of Indra.

One day, Indra had to fight a battle against Vritrasura, an extremely powerful demon. Indra went to Vishnu for help. Vishnu advised him to make a weapon from Dadhichi Muni's bones and use that to kill Vritrasura. Dadhichi Muni gladly donated his bones to Indra who used the weapon to kill Vritrasura. However, after killing Vritrasura, Indra was engulfed with guilt and to repent for his actions he disappeared from his heavenly home.

The devatas were worried about who would take charge of the kingdom of heaven. Soon they chose Sage Nahusha who had performed a hundred Ashwamedha yagyas and was tutored by the great Sage Vashishtha. But Nahusha soon became arrogant and proposed to marry Shachi. Sachi sought the advice of Sage Brihaspati. Brishaspati concocted a clever plan and asked Sachi to accept Nahusha's proposal on condition that he should arrive after 15 days in a palanquin carried by the eight greatest sages of the world. Sachi spent those 15 days in search of Indra. She finally found him meditating inside a lotus under water, atoning for his sin of killing Vritrasura, a Brahmin.

As the eight sages carried Nahusha in the palanquin, he kicked Sage Agastya urging him to move faster, and screamed, "Sarpa, Sarpa!" Aghast, Sage Agastya cursed him, "Become a Sarpa."

King Nahusa, now a python, fell on Earth. Sachi and Indra reclaimed their places as the king and queen of heaven and the world was restored to normalcy.

Indumati

From Ramayana, Raghuvamsha

Indumati was an apsara who had been cursed by a sage to be born on Earth. She was born as the princess of Vidarbha. The king of Vidarbha, Bhoja, had organised a swayamvar for his beloved sister. Brave princes from far and wide had gathered to win Indumati's hand in marriage. Indumati entered the hall holding a garland to put around the neck of her desired prince. Her friend Sunanda briefed her about every prince as she walked past them. However, none of the princes present seemed to impress Indumati. At last, one prince captured her attention – Prince Aja from Ayodhya. He belonged to the Ikshvaku dynasty. Indumati put the garland around his neck.

The other princes turned green with envy. They attacked Prince Aja, but the warrior prince used his celestial weapons to defeat them. The young couple reached Ayodhya, where Prince Aja's father, King Raghu, was overjoyed to see the bride. Soon, Aja became the king of Ayodhya and the couple had a baby boy, whom they named Dasharatha. Dasharatha would go on to become the father of Sri Rama.

One day, Aja and Indumati were walking in their palatial gardens when a garland fell on her from the heavens. The garland landed with such force that she instantly died. The curse had ended; the apsara left Earth and returned to her heavenly abode.

On being separated from his beloved companion, Aja started lamenting. Sage Vashishtha, the king's family preceptor, consoled him by advising him not to grieve like a common man.

Jahnava Devi
From Caitanya Caritamrita

Jahnava Devi was the daughter of Suryadasa Sarakhel, brother of Gauridasa Pandit—an intimate associate of Chaitanya Mahaprabhu. Jahnava Devi and her sister Vasudha were the incarnations of Revati and Varuni, who were the wives of Balarama.

Nityananda Prabhu was the incarnation of Balarama in Kali Yuga, and Chaitanya Mahaprabhu was the incarnation of Krishna. They appeared in Ekachakra, a small village in Bengal about 500 years ago. From the age of twelve, Nityananda Prabhu travelled with a mendicant sanyasi as his assistant. For many years, he travelled the length and breadth of the country and finally met Chaitanya Mahaprabhu at the age of 32. Chaitanya was only 20 years old. When he returned to Bengal, he met Suryadas Sarakhel and his two beautiful daughters. The moment Jahnava Devi and Vasuda saw Nityananda, they immediately felt their previous lives' connection and agreed to marry him. Vasudha gave birth to two children—Gangadevi and Virabhadra. After the birth of their two children, Vasudha left this world and Jahnava Devi raised both the children as her own.

Jahnava Devi went on to become one of the foremost preachers of Krishna consciousness in the whole of Bengal and embodied all the ideals of devotion in her being. She became the guru of the most powerful personalities in Bengal in that era. It is believed that she left the world by entering the Deity of Gopinath in Vrindavan.

Jambavati

From Bhagavat Purana, Shiv Purana

Daughter of the King of Bears, Jambavan, Jambavati became one of the most prominent queens of Dwarka after her marriage to Krishna. She was the second of the eight principal queen consorts of Krishna. However, her marriage to Krishna was accidental.

Krishna was searching for a jewel, Syamantaka, that had spoiled his reputation. The mystical gem had been gifted by the god Surya to his devotee, Satrajit, governor of the Yadava clan. The gem had such a dazzle that when Satrajit returned to Dwarka, he was sparkling so much that the people of Dwarka thought it was the Sun God himself. Krishna suggested that he give the precious diamond to the king of Mathura and his grandfather, Ugrasena. Instead, Satrajit gifted the precious jewel to his brother, Prasena. One day, Prasena was attacked by a lion when he was hunting in the forest. Everyone believed that Krishna had killed him for the jewel.

Krishna was horrified by the false allegation and set out to find Prasena. He followed the trail into the forest, where he found Prasena's dead body. Next, he followed the lion's trail and reached a cave, where he found Jambavan's son playing with the jewel. Jambavan and Krishna fought each other for a few weeks. Only when Jambavan realised that the one he was fighting was Krishna, the reincarnation of Rama whom he served in Treta Yuga, did he end the fight. He begged for forgiveness and offered the jewel to Krishna. He also offered his daughter's hand in marriage to Krishna. Krishna accepted the proposal and Jambavati became the queen of Dwarka. Her first-born child, Samba, was born from the blessings of Lord Shiva.

Kaikeyi
From Ramayana

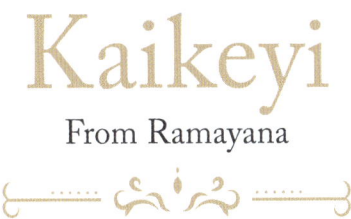

Kaikeyi was the dearest daughter of King Ashwapati of the Kekeya province. She was born right before her mother was sent to exile. She was raised by her hunchbacked nursemaid called Manthara, who exerted significant influence over her. Kaikeyi was a fierce woman who was raised alongside seven brothers. She was married to King Dasharatha on the condition that her son would be the next king of Ayodhya. Though her father had imposed that condition, it was unknown to Kaikeyi herself. She went on to become the favourite queen of Dasharatha. She often accompanied him on war expeditions and took the reins of his chariot in her hands. In fact, she once saved his life by putting her life at risk. A happy Dasharatha then gave her two boons, which she could ask for at any point in time.

When Dasharatha chose Rama as his heir, Kaikeyi was delighted, as she loved Rama as her own son. However, Manthara poisoned her mind and influenced her to use her two wishes. With one boon, Kaikeyi asked that her son Bharata be crowned the king and with the second boon she asked to send Rama to exile for 14 years. Although she did this to secure her position in the king's court and make her son the king, things did not go according to her plan. Dasharatha despised her until his dying breath. The entire kingdom hated her and her own son, Bharata chastised her. Ironically, the boons she got while saving Dasharatha's life became the reasons for his death.

When she realised the grave mistake she had made, she was willing to undo it. She went along with her son to Chitrakoot to beg Rama to return. However, Rama never blamed Kaikeyi for anything. He always loved and respected Kaikeyi like her own mother and even convinced Bharata to forgive her.

Kannagi
From Silapathikaram

Kannagi, the protagonist in the Tamil epic, Silapathikaram, was a chaste and courageous woman who remained with her husband despite his unfaithfulness. Kannagi was happily married to a wealthy merchant named Kovalan. Although Kannagi was beautiful and loving, Kovalan met a dancer, Madhavi and fell in love with her. He left Kannagi to have an affair with Madhavi. He showered Madhavi with expensive gifts until he spent all his wealth. When he had nothing left to give her, his eyes opened to the disaster he was facing. Feeling ashamed, he went back to his wife, Kannagi, who welcomed him with open arms.

They decided to leave the city and rebuild their lives in Madurai. Kannagi had an expensive gem-studded pair of anklets, which she gave Kovalan to sell and start his trading business.

The Madurai king's wife had lost an anklet that was very similar to Kannagi's anklet. When Kovalan went to the market to sell his wife's anklet, he was wrongly accused of stealing the queen's anklet. The royal guards acted in haste, beheading Kovalan for a crime he did not commit.

When Kannagi learnt about the gruesome death of Kovolan, she stormed into the king's court and showed the difference between her anklet and the queen's anklet. One was made of pearls, the other of ruby. Realising the error of judgement, the king and the queen died of shame. But that did not pacify Kannagi's anger. She cursed the entire city to burn away. Her curse fructified, and the city blazed for many days, causing great economic loss. She withdrew the curse at the request of the goddess Meenakshi.

Kannagi is praised for her chastity, forgiveness, strength and her refusal to tolerate injustice in the name of law.

Kaushalya
From Ramayana

Kaushalya was the eldest wife of King Dasharatha, and the queen of Ayodhya. Though a queen, she did not have the love of King Dasharatha, who loved and favoured his third wife Kaikeyi. Aware that her husband did not love her, Kaushalya chose to focus on self-growth.

She did not have a child for a long time. Finally, Dasharatha performed the Putrakameshti yagna, which yielded a pot of nectar. He divided the nectar amongst his wives and gave almost half the pot of nectar to Kaushalya. She drank it and prayed for a virtuous child as great as the king of the universe. Soon, Kaushalya gave birth to Rama, the incarnation of Lord Vishnu. Though she was the mother of Rama, Kaushalya loved all the other boys just as much. She especially loved Bharata, the son of Kaikeyi.

After her son's exile, she supported her husband even though it pained her heart. She loved Bharata and did not detest him when he was crowned as the king. After Bharata gave up the throne, Kaushalya acted as the Queen Dowager until Rama's return to Ayodhya. She was loved and adored by her people and widely regarded as the Queen Mother.

Kaushaki

From Matsya Purana, Shiva Purana

Kaushaki is a fierce goddess who emerged from the skin of Goddess Parvati. Once, Goddess Parvati was meditating to find ways to save the world from the demon brothers Shumbha and Nishumbha. The two demons had a boon from Brahma that they could not be killed by a male of any species and could die only die at the hands of a woman. They tortured saints, sages, well as devatas. They threatened everyone to only worship from thereon.

The devatas prayed fervently to the higher powers to come to their rescue and save them from the atrocities of the demon duo. Their desperate appeals were heard by Goddess Parvati. While meditating, her skin peeled off and the goddess Kaushaki emerged from within. Kaushaki's goal was to slay the two evil demons terrorising the Universe. She had eight arms, each holding weapons like trishula and chakra.

She was a mighty warrior goddess who looked menacing accompanied by a lion or tiger. She defeated the entire army of the demons single-handedly. Staring at defeat, the demon brothers sent their two assistants, Chanda and Munda. After killing them, she got the name Chamunda, the slayer of Chanda and Munda. Shumbha and Nishumba finally came face to face with Kaushaki, but they too perished, unable to face the fury of Kaushaki.

Kaveri

From Skanda Purana

Once, King Kavera was engrossed in penance when suddenly Lord Shiva appeared before him and said, "I bless you with a daughter who will help you in serving the kingdom and will also be the cause of your moksha." Soon, his wife gave birth to a beautiful daughter whom he named Kaveri. Kaveri was always eager to help people and assist her father in the welfare projects of the kingdom. When she grew up, Kaveri was married off to Sage Agastya, one of the most powerful sages of ancient India.

One day, a demon called Soorapadman mystically stopped rainwater from falling into the kingdom. Soon, all the water bodies dried. Kaveri was alarmed. Something had to be done or people would die.

At the same time, Sage Agastya had to travel out of the kingdom. He did not want to leave Kaveri behind while he made the long journey. So, he transformed her into water and kept her in his kamandala. While travelling, he came across a lake and put the kamandala near the bank to bathe in the almost empty river. Lord Ganesha transformed into a crow and pushed the kamandala. The water inside, which was Kaveri herself, flowed out happily.

She prayed to Lord Vishnu, asking to be turned into a holy river so that her father could attain moksha and liberate others who came to dip their sins in her holy waters.

Lord Vishnu said, "Ganga is holy because she arises from my feet. But you will be my garland and close to my heart."

Thus, Kaveri was considered as holy as Ganga. The Maharshis named the river 'Dakshina Ganga' (Ganga of the South).

Kripi
From Mahabharata

Saradvan was a sage, but unlike other sages, he loved archery. He performed penances like a sage, but always kept a bow and arrows by his side. His personality confused everyone, including the gods. Indra became insecure, worrying that the sage was accumulating special prowess through both brahminical and Kshatriya means. To break his tapasya, he sent an apsara named Janapadi to woo him. The sage fell in love with her and lost all his powers. The couple married and had twins, a boy and a girl. The boy was named Kripa and the girl child was called Kripi. Eventually, Kripa became the guru of King Shantanu of Hastinapur and his sister, Kripi, stayed with him.

Many years later, a fiery sage, Dronacharya, walked into the kingdom of Hastinapur. He was very similar to their father, as he performed tapasya like a Brahmin and was an expert in using weapons like a Kshatriya. Kripa felt that he would be the ideal match for his sister Kripi and arranged their marriage. Soon, Kripi gave birth to a son named Ashwatthama. Her son was born with a special jewel on his forehead, indicating that he would never be defeated in war. Although that jewel made the child special, their poverty made their life difficult. Drona and Kripi were always struggling to make ends meet. One day, Kripi asked her husband to go and fetch some money to feed their child some milk. She reminded him of his friendship with King Drupada. Drona went to meet him and returned with nothing but insults. Thus began a lifelong enmity which ended in the death of both Drona and Drupada in the battle of Kurukshetra.

Krishna and the Women

From Srimad Bhagavatam

Once Krishna was herding his cows in the forests of Vrindavan with his friends. As they took care of the cows, they also played many games. After a while, the boys felt hungry and requested Krishna to arrange some food for them. Krishna sent two of the boys to a Brahmin's house where many Brahmins were performing a fire sacrifice. When the boys asked them to give them food, they refused. They said that the food was an offering to the Supreme Lord and they cannot give it away to the boys.

The Brahmins did not realise, in their arrogance, that God himself was asking for the food. Disappointed, the boys returned to Krishna. Krishna smiled upon hearing what happened and asked his friends to approach the Brahmins' wives this time. The moment the wives heard that Krishna had sent the boys, they hastily brought all the food they had cooked for the yajna. They did not worry about their husbands' reaction. When the wives reached Krishna with all the food and offered it to him, Krishna smiled and accepted it. He suggested they return home and continue with their duties. He blessed them with auspiciousness. When they reached home, they found that their husbands were ashamed, as they could not see the truth that their wives could see.

The wives showed the kindness and faith that the prestigious Brahmins could not. They could see what was right in front of them. Their husbands felt as if it would take them an entire lifetime to cultivate the faith that their wives had.

Kubja
From Srimad Bhagavatam

Kubja was a hunchbacked woman from Mathura who was ugly to look at but had a golden heart. She made the best sandalwood paste in the whole of the city. She was so good at creating scents and pastes that the king of Mathura, Kamsa himself, used only her perfumes and oils.

One day, Krishna and Balaram entered Mathura along with their friends. The moment Kubja set her eyes on Krishna, she lost her heart. Being ugly, she was hesitant in approaching the divine looking Krishna, but Krishna spotted Kubja. She had stepped out of her house carrying freshly ground sandalwood paste to offer to Kamsa. Half of her body was bent forward, and she held one hand on her back to ease the backache. Due to discomfort, the movement of her body remained awkward. In her other hand, she carried a plate of sandalwood paste, the aroma of which spread to the other end of the street.

When Krishna drew in the heavenly fragrance, he was instantly attracted towards Kubja to take some of her sandalwood paste for himself. Kubja promptly offered all the paste to him. With great love, she beautified Krishna by applying the sandalwood paste on his limbs. Krishna was so grateful to her for her devotion and love that he decided to reciprocate. He placed his feet on her feet and placed the index finger of his right hand below her chin, lifting it upwards. The pressure caused Kubja to straighten up, and in the very next moment she was standing erect. Her hunch was gone and her facial features changed completely. Her purity and devotion turned her into a beautiful young woman.

Kunti

From Mahabharata

King Shurasena, a great Yadava ruler, had a son named Vasudeva, and a daughter named Prutha. His cousin, King Kuntibhoja of the Bhoja dynasty, was childless. Kuntibhoja requested Shurasena to let him take Prutha as his daughter. The king obliged and Prutha became the daughter of Kuntibhoja, who renamed her Kunti. Kunti grew up to become a very intelligent and extremely confident girl. When she was a teenager, Durvasa Muni came to stay at the palace for a few days. Her father appointed Kunti to take complete care of the needs of the sage. When the sage left, he was so pleased with her that he blessed her with a mantra with which she could invite any god she desired.

She was so thrilled with that blessing that she wanted to try its power. She invoked the Sun God who gave her a son. The young Kunti panicked as the baby was born out of wedlock. Fearing for her reputation, she put the child in a basket and left him in the river. He was eventually brought up by a chariot driver who named him Karna.

Kunti got married to Pandu and became the queen of Hastinapura. When Pandu got to know about Kunti's boon, he asked her to invoke the gods. Thus, the five illustrious Pandavas were born with the blessing of the most powerful gods. After the death of Pandu and his second wife Madri, Kunti raised all their sons to be the greatest proponents of dharma. She set the perfect example for them by her devotion to Krishna and her adherence to truth.

Lakshmana

From Bhagavat Purana, Vishnu Purana

Lakshmana, also known as Lakshana, was one of the eight principal queens of Krishna in Dwarka. She was born to the king of Madra and possessed many good qualities. Her beautiful smile enchanted many hearts, and she was fondly referred to as Charuhasini (one with a lovely smile). When she reached a marriageable age, her loving father organised a Swayamvar. It was attended by kings from far and wide, hoping to win Lakshmana's hand in marriage. The elite list included kings like Jarasandha, Duryodhana, Arjuna, and Krishna.

While some stories suggest that Krishna abducted Lakshmana and married her, others give a different account. Jarasandha and Duryodhana missed the targets completely in the archery contest, and Arjuna missed intentionally to allow Krishna to win her hand. Bhima abstained from participating as a mark of respect to Krishna. Krishna hit the target and won the bride's hand in marriage. Together they had ten sons - Praghosa, Gatravan, Simha, Bala, Prabala, Urdhvaga, Mahashakti, Saha, Oja and Aparajita.

Lakshmana herself narrates the exciting tale of her wedding to Draupadi when Krishna and his queens visit Hastinapur to meet the Pandavas.

Lakshmi

From Srimad Bhagavatam

Lakshmi is the goddess of wealth and prosperity. She also represents hard work, devotion, virtues and values. Lakshmi's four hands represent health, wealth, virtue and happiness. Lakshmi is seen in two forms: Bhudevi and Sridevi. Bhudevi represents the material energy, which refers to Mother Earth. Sridevi, on the other hand, represents the spiritual energy called Prakriti.

It so happened that the devas and the asuras and demons were involved in a joint project. Together, they were churning the ocean to obtain nectar. Soon, the ocean threw up many gifts from its depth. What, or rather who, emerged next caused a great deal of excitement. It was the beautiful Lakshmi Devi, daughter of the ocean. As soon as Lakshmi stepped out, her eyes fell on Vishnu Deva. Instantly, she felt drawn towards his electric blue complexion and charming, confident personality. Someone handed her a lotus garland with the instruction, "This is your swayamvar. Choose your husband, lovely lady."

Vishnu's transcendental qualities made him the most desirable. After full deliberation, Lakshmi, the goddess of fortune, accepted Vishnu as her husband. She blushed as she put her garland on him and he smiled at her.

Lakshmi epitomises the ideal woman, an independent individual. She chose Vishnu, the protector, over humans, gods and demons, stating that she wished her husband to be hard-working. If her devotees resort to vices like laziness, she does not bless them and leaves at once.

Lankini
From Ramayana

When Hanuman reached the gates of Lanka to rescue Sita Mata, he was rudely stopped by a horrendous demoness called Lankini. Nobody could enter Lanka without her sanction. She refused to let Hanuman enter the city when he asked politely, forcing Hanuman to take an aggressive stance.

Lankini rushed toward the little Vanara and shoved him away from the gate with great force. Her speed caught him off guard, and he found his tiny frame hurled a great distance away. He clenched his fist, ran towards the towering demoness, leaped into the air, and landed a hard punch across her jaw with his left fist. Lankini's gigantic body plopped to the ground, knocked out by a single punch. A minute later, a dazed and wrecked Lankini pulled herself up. Now, standing in front of Hanuman, was a humble demoness with folded palms, begging for mercy.

Lankini confessed that, in her previous life, she was a guard at Lord Brahma's abode. While being there, she was so consumed by the power of position that she attracted his curse. He banished her to life as a gatekeeper in Lanka where her ego would be purified over time by coexisting with larger egos. She would be liberated from the curse the day a vanara arrived in Lanka and punched her. She thanked Hanuman for freeing her from the curse and predicted the fall of Lanka. A single moment of association with Hanuman transformed Lankini so much more than wisdom from a thousand books ever could.

Lopamudra
From Mahabharata

Agastya Rishi assembled the most beautiful elements of creation and created a beautiful girl child who would grow up to be an outstanding scholar, an amazing poet, and a seer. He named the child Lopamudra as she was the quintessence of everything beautiful in this world. He handed over the baby to the childless king of Vidharbha, who was desirous of having a child. When Lopamudra was of marriageable age, Agastya came to Vidharbha to ask for her hand in marriage. The king was reluctant, but after Lopamudra expressed her eagerness to marry the sage, he obliged and the two got married. When Agastya brought her to his humble hermitage, she expressed her desire to have some comfort and luxury. The sage loved her dearly and decided to do everything in his power to get enough wealth that would make her happy.

He asked several kings if they had extra wealth that they could spare, but none of them had any. Then he went to meet Ilavala and Vatapi, two demon brothers, who robbed innocent men of their wealth and ate them up. Agastya managed to trick and eliminate them. The insurmountable amount of wealth that he managed to recover from them made Lopamudra very happy.

Agastya asked Lopamudra if she wished to have a thousand sons or one son who had the strength of a thousand men. Lopamudra immediately chose to have one son who would have the ability of a thousand. Thus, Dridhasyu was born, whom Lopamudra raised to be as kind and knowledgeable as her.

Madalasa
From - Markandeya Purana

Madalasa's life serves as an inspiration to motherhood and a mother's contribution to leading her children on the path to liberation.

Madalasa was a liberated soul. She married King Ritadhwaja as gratitude for saving her from the demons who attacked her. After marriage, her first son Vikranta was born. From his very birth, she taught him lessons on detachment, self-control, the futility of the material world, and the true nature of the soul. Even the lullabies she sang to him were about the five elements composing the body and the relationship between body and soul.

Vikranta grew up to be extremely saintly and renounced the world without getting married. He was followed by his brothers, Subahu and Shatrumardana, who also renounced worldly pleasures as soon as they reached adulthood.

When her fourth son Alarka was born, Ritadhwaja, requested his wife not to impart any spiritual knowledge to him, but rather educate him to be a wise ruler.

Madalasa raised Alarka with the highest standards of morality. She moulded him into an influential leader who went on to become a great king.

Alarka ruled the kingdom prosperously for many years and then renounced the world. Madalasa was a pillar of support for her husband and sons. Her husband, too, walked the spiritual path under her guidance.

Madhavi

From Mahabharata

King Yayati had a daughter called Madhavi. Madhavi's life had many difficulties, but she suffered all of it with utmost calm and poise, forgiving everyone, including her father, for the injustice done to her.

Sage Galava once asked King Yayati for eight hundred rare horses that were white with one black ear. The horses were a gift for Sage Vishwamitra. It was impossible for King Yayati to fulfil the demand for these rare horses. But turning away a sage empty-handed would be disastrous, so he offered Sage Galava his daughter, Madhavi.

Madhavi gave birth to four sons. Then she returned to her father. Yayati wanted to get her married, but she refused and became an ascetic. She had no interest in the affairs of the world.

Years later, Yayati died and went to heaven for a very short period and was soon expelled from there. He wandered in the forests on earth when one day he spotted Madhavi. Madhavi felt sorry for her father. She requested her four sons, who were now kings, to give away a fraction of their pious merits. However, they all refused. They held a grudge for Yayati's act of giving away their mother to a sage. But Madhavi had forgiven her father. She explained to her sons the futility of anger and hatred. The four kings were inspired by their mother and finally decided to give away some of their pious merits to their grandfather. Yayati blessed his daughter profusely and returned to heaven.

Madri
From Mahabharata

Madri was a princess of the Madra kingdom and the sister of King Shalya. Shalya once met the king of Hastinapura, Pandu, in the forest. The two became good friends, as they were impressed by each other. Bhishma believed Madri to be a suitable bride for Pandu, as she was revered for her beauty throughout the land. He travelled to Madra to ask for Madri's hand in marriage. Bhishma presented the king with wealth, gold, horses and elephants and got the hand of Madri for Pandu.

On a hunting trip, Pandu accidentally killed a sage who cursed him in return. Driven with guilt and remorse, Pandu left the kingdom to live in the forest in an attempt to repent for his sins. Unwilling to live in the palace without their husband, his two wives, Kunti and Madri, followed him. Kunti had a boon that allowed her to get a child from any god. She extended that boon to Madri and Madri called upon the twin gods Ashwini Kumars to get twin sons, Nakula and Sahadeva.

When Pandu died, Madri had no desire to live. She requested Kunti to take care of her sons so that she could follow Pandu in death. Kunti respected her wishes and became an exemplary mother to all of Pandu's sons.

Maitreyi

From Brihadaranyaka Upanishad

Born to Mitra Rishi, Maitreyi showed interest in learning the Shastras right from her childhood. At a very young age, she became disinterested in the material things and attempted to reach a stage of spiritual purity. She wanted to further her spiritual perfection by marrying the Sage Yajnavalkya. She was so spiritually strong that after marriage, she contributed to her husband's spiritual enhancement by broadening his perspective.

It is said that such was her spiritual personality that she enhanced Yajnavalkya's spiritual stature, knowledge, and growth. She herself gained from Yajnavalkya the spiritual knowledge necessary for liberation from the cycle of birth and death.

One day, Yajnavalkya confided in Maitreyi that he wanted to give up the worldly life. He then distributed his possessions between her and his other wife, Katyayani. Maitreyi asked him if having his possessions would help her become immortal, and if it would, why Yajnavalkya would leave it behind. Yajnavalkya was very happy with her argument. This led to a profound dialogue between the two about atman, Brahman and their equivalence, which became famous. It is part of the Brihadaranyaka Upanishad. After getting the insight of Yajnavalkya on Atma, Maitreyi attained supreme bliss.

Maitreyi is the perfect example of attaining supreme knowledge by simply hearing and following the Vedic path. She refused her husband's wealth and decided to share his knowledge instead. Maitreyi also composed ten of the thousand hymns in the Rig Veda.

Mandavi

From Ramayana

Sita's father, King Janak, had a younger brother, Kushadhwaja. Kushadhwaja was devoted to his brother, Janak. He had two daughters named Mandavi and Shrutakirti.

The entire family gathered in Mithila for Sita's swayamvar. When Rama broke the bow and won Sita's hand, the entire family rejoiced. King Dasharatha arrived from Ayodhya for the grand wedding ceremony along with Sage Vashishtha. Sage Vashishtha and Sage Vishwamitra had a meeting and proposed that the four sons of King Dasharatha would be a grand match for the four daughters of King Janak and Kushadhwaja. Kushadhwaja's daughters Mandavi and Shrutakirti were virtuous and cultured girls. The proposal was unanimously accepted with eagerness and excitement. One wedding turned into four weddings. Bharata tied the knot with Mandavi and Shatrughna married Shrutakirti.

Bharata and Mandavi had two sons, Taksha and Pushkala. Mandavi was always supportive of her husband. When Bharata constructed a small ashram at Nandi Grama and remained there, worshipping Rama's lotus feet, Mandvi spent her time meditating on Rama's holy name. She spent the rest of her life serving the mothers Kaushalya, Sumitra and Kaikeyi.

Mandodari

From Ramayana

Mandodari was the daughter of Hema Apsara and Mayasura, the asura master architect. She had two brothers-Dundubhi and Mayavi, both of whom were killed by Vali. Mandodari was married to Ravana and lived in Lanka for the rest of her life. Being the daughter of Apsara Hema, she was extremely beautiful. When Hanuman came to Lanka, he mistook her to be Sita when he saw Mandodari in Ravana's bedroom. Ravana, too, was totally mesmerised by her beauty.

Although Mandodari had a demon husband, she was of moral character. Ravana was an extremely selfish and evil person, while Mandodari was very virtuous and kind-hearted. She had three sons named Meghanad, Atikaya and Akshaya Kumar.

Mandodari constantly chastised Ravana for kidnapping Sita and wanted him to free her from captivity. She warned him that Rama was God himself and he should not challenge him. She would urge him repeatedly to follow the path of goodness, but all her advice fell on deaf ears. Despite everything, she remained loyal to Ravana. On Ravana's death, when she saw his many heads and limbs scattered on the battlefield, she could not help but explode with anger. Her anger was directed not at the killer of her husband, but at Ravana himself. His pride had led him to a death so undignified that his numerous body parts were scattered and being eaten by vultures.

Mirabai

From Rajasthani Folklore

Mirabai was born in a small village in Rajasthan, sometime in the early 16th century.

Being a Rajput princess, she grew up in a strong Vaishnava environment. When she was three years old, a sadhu gave her an idol of Krishna which totally enamoured her. One day, she was watching a wedding procession where she saw the bridegroom. She innocently asked her mother, "Mother, who will be my bridegroom?" Her mother pointed out to the idol of Sri Krishna and said, "Sri Krishna is your bridegroom." This inspired Mira's love for Krishna and she started spending all her time in worshipping his idol.

Mira was married at a tender age. After marriage, she refused to worship the family goddess Durga. She visited Krishna's temple every day. Her in-laws did not approve of her devotion to Krishna. They spoilt her reputation and even tried to poison her. They harassed her continuously, but she remained unharmed, as her beloved Krishna was always by her side.

Saddened by her husband's family, she wrote a letter to Saint Tulsidas asking for his advice. He convinced her that her relationship with Krishna was pure. Inspired by his letter, she left Rajasthan and walked barefoot through the scorching deserts to reach Vrindavan where she was acknowledged as a sincere devotee of Krishna. Her fame spread wide.

Till this day, Mira is an inspiration and an example of how to love God. The thousands of bhajans she wrote are loving offerings to Krishna, which are still very popular.

Mirabai will always be remembered for her love for Krishna and the soulful songs she wrote in his devotion.

Mitravinda

From Bhagavat Purana, Vishnu Purana

Mitravinda was the sixth of the Ashtabharya (the eight principal queens of Krishna). She was the daughter of King Jayasena of Avanti. She was also known as Shaibya, as she was a descendent of the pious King Shibi. She was an extremely noble and beautiful girl.

Her brothers Vinda and Anuvinda were friends of Duryodhana, the eldest of the Kauravas. They disliked Krishna and the Pandavas, who were rivals of Duryodhana. However, Mitravinda was in love with Krishna. They organised a Swayamvara for her and asked her to choose Duryodhana as her groom. An alliance with Duryodhana would strengthen the kingdoms. The brothers did not even bother to invite Krishna and Balarama.

When Balarama got to know about their exclusion from the Swayamvara, he got upset. He was aware of Vinda's and Anuvinda's actual intentions. He also knew that Mitravinda wanted to marry Krishna. He asked Krishna to attack Avanti and abduct Mitravinda. Before making any move, Krishna wanted to ensure that Mitravinda really wanted to marry him. He sent his sister Subhadra to meet Mitravinda and know her wishes. Subhadra returned to confirm Mitravinda's love for Krishna and her request to abduct and save her from her brothers.

Krishna swung into action and stormed the Swayamvar with his army. He abducted Mitravinda, defeating Duryodhana and all the princes who tried to stop him. Krishna took Mitravinda back to Dwarka, where they got formally married.

Mohini Murti

From Srimad Bhagavatam

Mohini Murti was the incarnation of Lord Vishnu himself. He had assumed the form of this beautiful woman who could hypnotise anyone with her mesmerising looks. Vishnu took the form of Mohini to mesmerise and distract the demons from the pot of nectar churning the ocean. As Mohini, he captured the hearts of demons who voluntarily handed over the nectar in order to win her favour. Mohini took the pot from the demons and distributed the juice of immortality to the devas while the demons stared at her helplessly. She was so beautiful that when Lord Shiva heard about Lord Vishnu incarnating as Mohini, he became eager to see this form. He rushed from Kailash on his bull, along with his wife and disciples, to meet Lord Vishnu and urged him to present this mesmerising form of his.

Once, Mohini Murti saved Shiva from a demon called Bhasmasura. Bhasmasura had a boon from Shiva that anyone he touched would turn into ashes. After being granted the boon, the wicked demon ran to touch Shiva himself and turn the god into ashes. However, he encountered Mohini Murti on his way. Bewildered by her beauty, the demon stopped to talk to her. Mohini offered to teach him a dance form called Mukta-nritya. The demon jumped at the offer and followed all of Mohini's instructions. While dancing, he put his hand over his head and was reduced into ashes.

Mohini was not just exquisitely beautiful, but also clever, with a powerful presence of mind. She saved the gods many times, using her beauty and mind.

Narmada

From Skanda Purana

There are many legends surrounding the birth of the goddess Narmada. One legend says she was born when Shiva perspired while meditating. The perspiration collected in a tank, which flowed out as Narmada. Another legend attributes her birth to the tears of Brahma.

Once, Sage Markandeya was resting on the banks of Narmada. Yudhishthira and Draupadi arrived there and asked the sage why he chose to rest alongside the Narmada instead of other more significant holy places. The sage recounted the story of King Pururva, who was asked by the sages to bring Narmada to Earth and purify all earthly inhabitants. The king performed severe penances to please Lord Shiva. As his boon, the king requested Shiva to send Narmada on Earth. Shiva promptly instructed Narmada to descend on Earth. However, Narmada required a base to land on. Shiva directed Prayank, the son of Vindhyachal Mountain, to hold Narmada when she descended. With his help, Narmada descended on Earth, but her waters created a massive flood. The deities requested her to reduce in size and she minimised herself. Narmada blessed Pururva and liberated his ancestors from sin. After finishing his tale, Sage Markandeya told Yudhishthira that taking a dip in the Narmada is like performing the Ashwamedha yagna.

Once a year, Ganga visits Narmada to cleanse herself of the sins she has accumulated.

Parvati

From Shiva Purana

Parvati Devi, the divine consort of Lord Shiva, is the goddess of purity, nourishment, love, power and harmony. Born as the daughter of Himavat, she dedicated her early life in austerities to woo Lord Shiva. Impressed by her dedication, Shiva accepted her as his bride. Although Parvati shows her power and strength in times of crisis, riding a ferocious tiger, her heart is gentle and full of love.

One day, she spontaneously created a little boy from the turmeric paste she used to cleanse her body and named him Vinayak. Vinayak's round eyes matched his round, abdomen. Parvati asked her son to guard the gate while she went for a bath and not let anyone enter.

When Shiva returned, he encountered the strange boy who would not let him enter his own house. Furious with the boy's disrespect to him and other gods who tried to convince him to let Shiva enter, Shiva cut the boy's head off with his trident. Parvati stepped out, and saw her precious son's lifeless body. She demanded Shiva to restore Vinayak's life at once. Shiva immediately sent Nandi to bring a head to attach on Vinayak's neck. Nandi returned with an elephant's head and Shiva placed it on the dead boy's neck, breathing life into his lifeless body. After that, Vinayak came to be known as Ganesha.

Parvati was delighted to see her son alive, even if he had an elephant's head. Shiva blessed his son that he would be the master of all his followers and the most loved god in the world. That made Parvati, the universal mother, extremely satisfied.

Radha, Karna's Mother
From Mahabharata

Radha was a gentle woman of Hastinapura. Her husband, Adiratha, was the chariot driver of King Dhritarashtra. They did not have any children and not a day went by when Radha did not pray for a child in her lap.

Her prayer was answered one day. She was at the banks of River Ganga praying for a child, when a basket came floating towards her. To her awe and joy, there was a baby boy inside the basket. The couple quickly took the child home and raised him as their own son. They named him Vasusena- one who possessed natural wealth, since he was born with an armour on his body. The boy grew up loving his mother, not knowing that she did not give birth to him. Radha taught her son to be virtuous and kind.

The boy later came to be known as Karna. His love for Radha was such that he was also referred to as Radheya, or son of Radha. Radha had another son after Karna came and he was called Shon. Karna and Shon were very close and the four of them were a happy family. Radha's life revolved around her Radheya. Karna's bond with his mother was really strong. He never turned away from Radha, even after finding out that Kunti was his actual mother. She remained an inspiration to him for all his life.

Radharani

From Caitanya Caritamrita

Radha is the eternal consort of Lord Krishna. She is believed to be an incarnation of the Goddess Lakshmi. Radha is known for her love and devotion towards Krishna. She is believed to be the female counterpart of Krishna, who accompanies him in all of his incarnations.

Radha was the adopted daughter of Vrishabhanu. Vrishabhanu, the ruler of Barsana, once found a little baby girl on a lotus floating in the Yamuna river. Not able to find her parents, Vrishabhanu Maharaj brought the little effulgent baby home. His wife, Kirtida, was shocked to discover that the girl would not open her eyes. Not just that, she couldn't even hear, nor could she speak anything. They were childless for many years and were now blessed with this little baby. Unfortunately, the girl turned out to be blind, deaf and dumb.

One day, Nanda Maharaj visited their house with Yashoda and little Krishna. While the adults were busy socialising, little Krishna crawled into the room where Radha was in her cradle. Krishna stood up on his little feet, extended his soft hand into the cradle and touched Radha. With the first touch of Krishna, Radha opened her eyes and saw Krishna. Krishna's face was the first thing she saw in the world. Krishna uttered some broken words and his voice was the first sound Radha heard in this world. Then, from her mouth, she tried to speak the name of Krishna, and that was the first word she uttered from her mouth.

After that, Radha's life revolved only around Krishna. She used all her time and abilities to serve Krishna and make him happy. Radha is admired as the perfect lover. She has also inspired many forms of literary work and performance arts.

Rati - Wife of Kamadeva

From Srimad Bhagavatam

Rati is the goddess of love and consort of Kamadeva, the god of love. She was famous for her sensual beauty and accompanied Kamadeva on all his projects. She was also present with Kamadeva when the gods entrusted them to generate love in Lord Shiva's heart. It was a risky venture, but they had no other option. It was necessary for universal welfare that Shiva united with Parvati so that they could have children who could kill demonic forces.

Rati and Kamadeva reached Kailash and Kamadeva shot his arrows of flowers at Lord Shiva. No matter how many arrows he shot, there was no impact on Shiva. Then Parvati passed from there and Shiva opened his eyes. Taking this as his cue to shoot again, Kamadeva fired his arrow. Lo-and-behold, Shiva felt immense love rising in his bosom. Surprised at himself, he looked around to find Kamadeva lurking behind a bush. He was so angry that he opened his third eye and reduced Kamadeva to ashes.

When Rati saw her husband turned into ashes, she broke down inconsolably. She pleaded with Shiva to return him to life. The gods too descended and clarified that they had instructed Kamadeva to do what he had done. But Shiva's act was irrevocable. However, he felt sorry for Rati and promised her that Kamadeva would be born again as the son of Krishna and Rukmini and he would marry her again in Dwapar yuga.

Revati

From Srimad Bhagavatam

King Kakudmi could not find a suitable match for his exceptional daughter, Revati who wanted to marry the worthiest man on Earth. So Kakudmi went to Brahma loka to seek the help of Brahma. Seeing that Brahma was busy, Kakudmi and Revati waited.

When Brahma finally became free, 27 Chatur yugas had passed. Satya Yuga and Treta Yuga were over and Dwapara Yuga had begun on Earth. All the people he had left behind on Earth were long gone and Revati was thousands of years old by earthly standards. Kakudmi's kingdom and all his wealth were long gone. Dwapara Yuga was the Yuga of Lord Krishna. Brahma told Kakudmi that Krishna's brother Balarama would make the perfect match for Revati.

Kakudmi and Revati returned to Earth which had changed drastically. They reached Dwarka where they proposed marriage to Balrama. Revati was much taller than Balarama. Balarama solved the issue with his plough. He placed the plough on Revati's shoulder and pushed it downward. This reduced her height till it matched perfectly with Balarama's.

After all the hardships, Revati finally married the strongest man on Earth. She bore two sons and a daughter.

Rohini

From Srimad Bhagavatam

Rohini's story is not an ordinary one. It's a story about great sacrifices and great courage. She was the second wife of Vasudeva, the Yadava prince. While her husband and his other wife Devaki were imprisoned wrongfully by Kamsa, Rohini somehow escaped to Vrindavan. Though imprisoned, Vasudeva arranged for her safety in the house of Nanda Maharaj, who was his close friend.

Though Rohini's life was safe, she was painfully aware of the tribulations her husband and Devaki were undergoing in the prison cell. Seven years passed and something miraculous happened. One day, she heard the news from Mathura that Devaki's seventh pregnancy had ended in a miscarriage. But the previous night, Rohini had a special experience that she didn't share with anyone else except Yashoda and Nanda Maharaj. In the middle of the night, she suddenly felt a blue radiance engulf her body. She suddenly experienced great energy. The next moment, it all disappeared. But she felt something moving in her belly. That is when she realised that a baby had been deposited in her womb by a powerful force. When she heard of the termination of Devaki's pregnancy, she knew the child had been transferred from Devaki's womb to hers. Yoga Maya, the divine energy of the Supreme Lord, had arranged for this transfer. Since the embryo was attracted from Devaki's womb to Rohini's womb, the boy was eventually named Sankarshan, which means 'the attracted one'. He was also called Balarama, as he was the source of all the strength in this world. Rohini helped Yashoda raise the two children, Krishna and Balarama.

Rukmini

From Srimad Bhagavatam

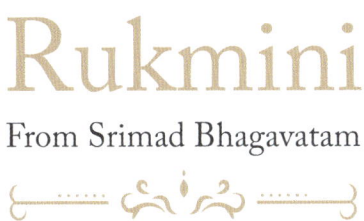

Rukmini was the daughter of King Bhismaka, the king of Vidarbha. She was an extremely intelligent and talented princess. Rukmini was also called Vaidharbhi by virtue of being the princess of Vidarbha.

When in court, she heard stories describing the glories of Krishna from hundreds of merchants, Brahmins, and travellers who came from Dwarka. Slowly, she formed an image of Krishna, which developed into love over time, till finally she decided that she would marry none other but him. This did not go down well with her brother Rukmi as he had already decided to send a proposal to Shishupala, the prince of Chedi, which would be a great political alliance. Rukmi did not like Krishna and went ahead, ignoring Rukmini's desire.

When marriage with Shishupala was declared against her wishes, she wrote a letter to Krishna, expressing her desire to marry him. She sent that letter with a Brahmin. The letter contained an entire plan that Krishna could adopt to kidnap her from her people without any bloodshed. When Krishna received that letter, he decided to follow her plan. On the day of the marriage, Krishna kidnapped Rukmini from right under the nose of her brother. A shocked Rukmi sent his army behind them, accompanied by Shishupala's army. Balarama, leading Dwarka's army, intervened and stopped the attack. Rukmini and Krishna married in Dwarka with great pomp and Rukmini became the queen of Dwarka.

Rukmini is the goddess of fortune, therefore also known as Sridevi. Where there is Krishna, there is his divine consort, Rukmini, too.

Ruma
From Ramayana

Ruma belonged to the Vanara clan and was the wife of Sugriva. Sugriva was the younger brother of Vali, king of Kishkindha. As Sugriva's wife, Ruma had a luxurious life in the royal palace. But things went drastically wrong one day when Sugriva returned after a long absence from home to inform her that Vali was dead. Since Vali's son Angad was young, the ministers crowned Sugriva as king. All was well till the unthinkable happened. Vali returned and went wild with rage, seeing Sugriva seated on the throne.

Ruma watched helplessly as Vali kicked Sugriva out of the kingdom and kidnapped her. She was kept captive in Vali's palace while she learnt from her sources that her husband Sugriva was running all over the world, hiding from Vali. One day, she was lost in thoughts when she heard Sugriva's voice. He was calling out to Vali, challenging him for a fight. Ruma was surprised because she knew her husband was no match for Vali. She wondered if there was someone powerful backing him.

Ruma felt a surge of hope. Maybe Sugriva would manage to overpower Vali and rescue her. She missed him and she missed her freedom. Her guess was right on target, as Sugriva had the backing of the all-powerful Lord Rama, who ultimately killed Vali as a gesture of friendship for Sugriva. Ruma was rescued and once again became the queen of Kishkindha.

Sachi Mata

From Srimad Bhagavatam

Sachi Mata was humility personified. Her entire life was dedicated to the service of Vishnu and the Vaishnavas. Despite hundreds of obstacles in her life, Sachi never faltered from the path of spirituality.

She was the only daughter of Pandit Nilambar Chakravarti. At a young age, she was married to Jagannatha Mishra, a famous scholar and astrologer of Navadvipa. They lived on the banks of the Ganga. The young couple had eight daughters, each of them died soon after birth. Finally, Sachi Mata's ninth child, a boy named Vishwarupa, was born. Twelve years later, another boy named Chaitanya was born. Both her sons accepted sanyasa at a young age. Her husband seeped in spirituality and her two daughters-in-law were the divine consorts of the Supreme Lord.

Her life was a series of tragedies; the successive loss of eight newborn infants, the death of her husband; her elder son accepting sanyasa; her daughter-in-law Lakshmipriya's untimely death; Nimai's sanyasa and the resultant abandonment of herself and her adolescent second daughter-in-law, Vishnupriya. Despite all the suffering, she continued her life of silent penance to support her son's mission.

Sachi Mata made many sacrifices throughout her life and her devotion to Chaitanya Mahaprabhu's mission was unparalleled. Despite the numerous obstacles in her life, Sachi never wavered from the path of spiritual.

Sarama

From Ramayana

Sarama was an unusual rakshasa woman in Lanka who went against Ravana to stand by her righteous and pious husband, Vibhishana. In Lanka, Vibhishana was often ridiculed for his faith and devotion to Lord Rama. Yet, Sarama remained loyal to him and followed the moral path herself. She always supported Vibhishana with her whole heart.

Sarama defied Ravana and became friends with Sita. She advised Sita on the ways to cope with the life-threatening situation Sita was facing and kept her spirits high at all times. She even brought to Sita confidential news and kept her updated on the details of the war between Rama and Ravana.

Before the war, Vibhishana had left Lanka to join Rama in his fight. Sarama stayed back to help him by sharing the ground realities of Lanka with him. With her help, Vibhishana could locate the secret location of the yagna performed by Ravana. With this information, Hanuman could disrupt the yagna and foil Ravana's plans of gaining invincible boons. In this way, Sarama played a significant role in the battle of good and evil, helping good win the war.

Her daughter Trijita was also a good-hearted demon who learnt compassion and goodness from her mother.

Saranya

From Rigveda, Markandeya Purana, Harivamsa, Matsya Purana

Saranya, also known as Sandhya, was a strong-willed woman married to Vivasvan, the sun god. They had two sons, Vivasvat Manu and Yama, and a daughter, Yamuna. Yama and Yamuna were twins.

Life was unusually tough for Saranya because of the scorching heat of her husband, the sun god. Things became so bad that Saranya decided to leave home. She did not want to hurt Vivasvan, so she created a lookalike from her shadow and sent her as a replacement. Chhaya, her lookalike, lived as Saranya without anyone finding out the truth.

One day, judging by Chhaya's strange behaviour, Vivasvan thought that something was wrong. He accosted Chhaya and forced her to tell the truth. Chhaya revealed that she was not Saranya. Vivasvan went looking for Saranya at his father-in-law Vishwakarma's house, who informed him that Saranya, unable to bear the suffocating heat, had come there but soon left for Uttara Kuru in the form of a mare.

When Vivasvan finally found Saranya as a mare, he transformed himself into a horse. Saranya was both surprised and delighted to see her husband. He also turned down his heat for her to be able to bear him. Together they spent some lovely moments in Uttara Kuru and two more sons were born to them, the twins Ashwini Kumaras — Nasatta and Dasra. The twins went on to become physicians of the gods. The extra energy that Vivasvan had shed was used in making a trident for Shiva and a chakra for Vishnu.

Saraswati

From Brahmanda Purana

Saraswati is the fountainhead of all wisdom. She is dressed in white and sits on a lotus. The colour white signifies purity, knowledge and divine wisdom. Water under her lotus seat symbolises a perennial flow of knowledge. Her four arms represent mind, intellect, intelligence and ego. They also represent the four Vedas, the most sacred books of Hindus. Swan is the carrier of Saraswati and possesses an incredible power of discrimination between the real and the unreal.

When Brahma Deva first created all the planets, there were no laws in existence. The planets did not know whether they should rotate or revolve or make their orbits long or short. Since every planet moved as per its whim, there was utter confusion.

Brahma sat down to meditate and a magnificent personality emerged from his mouth. Dressed in white, she radiated a soft glow. That was Saraswati, the goddess of knowledge, mother of the Vedas, and the inventor of Sanskrit. She was seated on a swan, holding a palm leaf manuscript in one hand and a musical instrument (vina) in the other. She exuded beauty in simplicity.

The melodious tune of her vina had a profoundly soothing effect on Brahma, and the roar of worldly commotions ceased to exist. Soon, the sun, moon and stars came into existence and the world organised itself in a sustainable pattern. The rivers and oceans became alive and the seasons swung into action. Everything fell into place. Saraswati became the source of wisdom for the creator, Brahma.

The wealth of knowledge bestowed by Saraswati is eternal.

Sati

From Shrimad Bhagavatam

Sati was the favourite child of Brahma's son, Daksha. Daksha had the responsibility of populating the Universe. All his daughters were married to sages and gods. But Sati, although his dearest daughter, went against his wishes.

Sati's heart was set on marrying Lord Shiva. But Shiva's unconventional appearance and lifestyle did not appeal to Daksha. Ignoring her father's wish, Sati went to the Himalayas to perform penance in order to please Lord Shiva. Instead of the comforts of her palace, she embraced severe austerities. Instead of opulent food, she ate one leaf a day. She braved the harsh weather to meditate on the one and only one Lord Shiva.

Shiva finally took notice of her austerities and appeared before her and consented to marry her. Soon they were married and Sati left to live with Shiva. Daksha did not take this lightly and cut her off from his family. He conducted a lavish yagya and purposely did not invite Sati or Shiva. Although furious, Sati still went to the yagya, thinking that a daughter does not need an invitation. But she had miscalculated the extent of her father's hatred for Shiva. He insulted Shiva in front of Sati and the huge gathering of guests. Unable to tolerate the heap of insults, Sati chose to give up her life. She invoked Agni, the fire god, and sacrificed herself in that fire.

Shiva, in his fury, beheaded Daksha. However, at Brahma's request, he brought him back to life by placing a goat's head on Daksha's neck. As the grief-stricken Shiva carried Sati's body all over the world, parts of her body fell to fifty-one places. Those places are now known as 'Shakti Peethas'. She is still worshipped today to attain marital bliss and longevity.

Satyabhama
From Srimad Bhagavatam

Satyabhama was the daughter of Satrajit, a very respectable citizen of Dwarka. Satrajit was a great devotee of the Surya the sun god who had given him a very precious jewel named Shayamantaka. The jewel magically produced 80 kilos of gold daily and ensured that the possessor of the jewel remained free from any disease, hunger or thirst.

Krishna felt that a priceless jewel like Shyamanataka should be in the possession of a monarch so that it may be used for the benefit of the society. Satrajit was using it only for his own personal enjoyment, so Krishna asked Satrajit to gift the jewel to Ugrasena, the king of Mathura.

Satrajit, however, refused and gave the jewel to his brother, Prasena. Prasena got killed by a lion in the forest and the jewel was lost. Satrajit blamed Krishna for Prasena's death, so he set out to prove his innocence. After retrieving the jewel from Jambawan, he presented the gem to Satrajit. Satrajit begged Krishna for forgiveness and offered his beautiful daughter Satyabhama's hand in marriage. He also gave the Shyamantaka jewel as a gift, but Krishna refused the jewel and only accepted Satyabhama as his wife.

Satyabhama loved Krishna and often travelled with him during military expeditions. In fact, she was a master at handling the bow and arrow. She helped him kill many demons, including Narakasura. Once, she went on an expedition to the heavens. There, she loved the flowers from the Parijata tree, which belonged to Indra. Krishna lifted the entire tree and brought it to Dwarka as a gift for Satyabhama.

Satyavati
From Mahabharata

Satyavati was the daughter of an apsara but raised by a fisherman. She inherited her mother's beauty. When the king of Hastinapur Shantanu saw her for the first time, he set his mind on marrying her. However, her father did not trust the king and put forth the condition that Satyavati's children should be crowned king. Shantanu already had a son, named Bhishma, who was heir to his throne. Shantanu had to refuse the fisherman's condition. Bhishma stepped in and took an oath that he would never marry and produce any offspring of his own. This way, Satyavati's children would easily become the future kings of Hastinapur.

With this vow, Bhishma ensured the marriage of his father to Satyavati. After Shantanu passed away, Bhishma appointed Satyavati's first-born child, Chitrangada, as king of Hastinapur. Sadly, the young king died fighting a war and the second son, Vichitraveerya, was appointed king. He, too, passed away within seven years.

Satyavati, along with Bhishma, managed the affairs of Hastinapura till her grandchildren could become kings. Her grandchildren were the blind Dhritarashtra, the sickly Pandu and the wise Vidura. Thus, Satyavati was the great grandmother of the Pandavas and the Kauravas.

She was also the mother of Rishi Vaishampayan, who later became famous as Ved Vyasa, author of Mahabharata and Srimad Bhagavatam. He wrote about his mother, Satyavati, who stepped in to manage the kingdom and took tough decisions much ahead of her times.

Savitri

From Mahabharata

Savitri was born to King Ashwapati of Madra from the boon of the sun god Savitr. Savitri was born out of devotion and asceticism, which she practised herself her entire life.

Savitri was an extremely beautiful and pious woman. When she reached a marriageable age, her father asked her to find a groom for herself. During her search, Savitri found Satyavan, who immediately captured her heart. He was the son of the exiled king Dyumatsena of the Salwa kingdom, who had also lost his sight and was now living with his wife and son as a forest dweller.

Narad Muni appeared before King Ashwapati to inform him that Satyavan was destined to die one year from now. Savitri overheard the conversation but despite her father's pleas, insisted on marrying Satyavan. Seeing her devotion, Narada Muni and her father gave her their blessings.

Savitri and Satyavan got married and lived in the forest with Satyavan's parents. One year passed in bliss and harmony. Savitri proves to be a dutiful wife and daughter-in-law. As the date grew closer, she performed intense austerities for Satyavan's life extension. On the day of his predicted death, Savitri accompanied Satyavan into the forest. Satyavan was cutting wood in the forest when he collapsed on Savitris's lap. Yamaraj arrived and took Satyavan away. Savitri silently and determinedly followed Yamaraj. Surprised, Yamaraj asked her to choose a boon. She chose to do good to her in-laws by regaining their lost kingdom. Yamaraj was impressed by her confidence and intelligence. He wanted to give her another boon and this time she asked to be a mother of a hundred children. Once that was granted, Yamaraj realised he was in a fix. He had to return Satyavan's soul with an extended long life. Thus, Savitri conquered death for her husband.

Shabari

From Ramayana

Shabari was born in a Nishada family that lived in the forest. She found shelter in the ashram of Matanga Rishi in the forest very far from where she lived. Matanga Rishi allowed her to stay there and serve them. With the association of Matanga Rishi, she practised intense austerities and progressed spiritually. She developed great veneration and respect for her guru and carried out all the tasks that were assigned to her with great diligence.

Many years later, Matanga Rishi told her he was leaving for higher realms along with his disciples and asked her to stay back in the ashram till Lord Rama came. Matanga Rishi told her she should serve Lord Rama, who would come one day searching for Mother Sita. Accordingly, Shabari waited for many years for the sage's prediction to come true. She had absolute faith in her teachers' words.

Every single day, she cleaned the ashram, plucked the most beautiful flowers, picked the most succulent fruits, made the most beautiful garlands, and kept everything perfect, ready to receive Lord Rama. She did this with so much faith that the Lord could come any day, any moment. When finally, after many years Sri Rama did come, Shabari served him so gently that it touched Rama's heart very much. In fact, Rama was so impressed by her devotion that he addressed her with many names, appreciating her various qualities. After a short period of association, she asked Rama if he was satisfied with her and if she had his permission to leave now so that she could reunite with her spiritual master. Rama offered his respects to this great soul who had so much faith in her guru and his instructions.

Shakuntala
From Mahabharata

Shakuntala was a woman of excellence. She inherited divine beauty from her apsara mother, Menaka, and superlative intelligence from her father Vishwamitra, a king turned sage. Menaka's intention in uniting with Vishwamitra was to distract him from his spiritual progress. When Vishwamitra found out, he was extremely angry at her and went back to his ascetic lifestyle. Menaka departed for her heavenly home too, leaving their young daughter to fend for herself in the forest.

Sage Kanva found the ethereally beautiful child surrounded by a group of Shakunta birds. He brought her home and called her Shakuntala. She grew up to be a treasure trove of virtue and grace. One day, King Dushyanta saw her in the ashram and fell head over heels in love with her. Shakuntala also felt attracted to him and they got married by exchanging garlands, as per the Gandharva tradition. Dushyanta gave her his signet ring as a token of their love before returning to his kingdom.

Before they could declare their marriage in public, Shakuntala was cursed by Durvasa Muni for failing to greet him with respect. Sage Durvasa cursed her that the person she was thinking of would forget about her altogether and get his memory back only when she showed them a personal token.

Because of the curse, Dushyanta could not remember her. She went through all the suffering with poise and dignity. The king finally got his memory back upon seeing the signet ring that he had given her. He rushed to the forest to find Shakuntala. He was surprised to see that he had a son, a brave boy named Bharata, who was playing with wild animals.

Shakuntala represents feminine strength that is assertive yet sacred, independent yet noble.

Shanta
From Ramayana

Shanta was the elder sister of Lord Rama. She was born much before Rama to Dasharatha and Kaushalya. When Shanta was young, Dasharatha's friend King Romapada visited Ayodhya. During his stay in the kingdom, he was mesmerised by this little girl and made an unusual request to Dasharatha. Despite being married for a long time, Romapada did not have a child of his own. He urged his friend to give her to him for adoption. Though he loved his little child, Dasharatha could empathise with his childless friend. He and Kaushalya decided to give their daughter to Romapada for adoption. Romapada took the little girl back to his kingdom and raised him in the most loving manner. In his care, Shanta grew up to become a beautiful and intelligent girl who was gentle and yet accomplished in all talents.

One day, while Romapada was busy talking to his daughter, a Brahmin approached him for some help. But the king was so absorbed in talking to his daughter that he neglected the Brahmin, who left disappointed. Indra, the god of rain, was very disappointed at the disrespectful attitude of Romapada and decided not to send rains to his kingdom. After 11 years of suffering from acute drought, Romapada finally discovered the solution in the form of another Brahmin named Rishi Shringa. With great effort, he managed to convince Rishi Shringa to come to his kingdom. The moment he stepped into the kingdom, torrential rainfall took place. The king was so grateful that he offered Shanta's hand in marriage, which Rishi Shringa accepted. The same Rishi Shringa performed the *putra kameshti* yagna for King Dasharatha, that resulted in him being blessed with four divine sons.

Shikhandi

From Mahabharata

In her past life, Shikhandi was Princess Amba born to the king of Kashi. She had been kidnapped by Bhishma who wanted her to get married to his step brother Vichitravirya. This humiliated Amba deeply, and she performed an intense penance. She left her body with the desire to take revenge on Bhishma during her next birth.

Amba was born again to King Drupada as Shikhandi. Drupada raised Shikhandi like a boy and she became skilled in warfare. After an accidental meeting with a Yaksha, she exchanged her gender with him and returned as a man. She fought the Kurukshetra war on the Panadavas' side to avenge the insult she faced in her last life by Bhishma.

In the war, Bhishma recognised Shikhandi as Amba and thought it was against his dharma to fight a battle with a woman. He lowered his weapons. Arjuna had expected this response and was hiding behind Shikhandi. As soon as Arjuna saw Bhishma lowering his weapons, he attacked him with a volley of high-powered arrows. In this way, Arjuna could bring down the invincible Bhishma with the help of Shikhandi. Thus, Shikhandi's revenge was complete, and the Pandavas gained a major win. Shikhandi was finally killed by Ashwatthama on the eighteenth day of the war. After Shikhandi's death, her masculinity was transferred back to the Yaksha.

Sita

From Ramayana

Sita was an incarnation of the goddess Lakshmi. She appeared from the Earth and was adopted by King Janak, the king of Mithila. She is also known as Bhumija, the daughter of Mother Earth. Sita was an extraordinary child and when she reached adulthood, Janak held a grand swayamwar to find her a suitable husband. The kings who attended it the swayamvar were asked to string the enormous bow of Lord Shiva to get Sita's hand in marriage. After many kings failed in their attempts to even lift the bow, Janak was disappointed. Just then, Vishwamitra entered with Rama and Lakshmana of Ayodhya. As soon as Rama and Sita saw each other, they fell deeply in love with each other. They knew that they were soulmates. Rama lifted the bow and, in his attempt to tie the string, cracked the mighty bow from its centre.

Sita had a strong and determined personality. When Rama was exiled to the forest, he was reluctant to take Sita with him, but Sita fought her way out, refusing to stay behind. She withstood the hardships of forest life without once complaining about the lack of luxuries. She loved to be amidst nature and enjoyed every day in the forest with Rama, as if it were a picnic. Her heart was so soft that in her presence, Rama could not kill any demon. Her compassion was so great that she even forgave the one-eyed demonesses who tortured her for ten months in Ashoka Vatika.

Sita represents bhakti. When Hanuman found her in Lanka, he received many blessings from her.

Subhadra
From Mahabharata

Subhadra was the daughter of Vasudeva and the sister of Krishna and Balaram. She was born much after Kamsa was killed and thus did not experience the traumatic childhood that her brothers had to experience with death constantly hovering above them. When Subhadra grew to a marriageable age, Krishna then set up the plan in which Arjuna disguised himself as a sanyasi and stayed with them in Dwarka. Subhadra was engaged in serving him for that entire period. Soon she fell in love with Arjuna.

Balaram initially opposed the marriage, as he had already promised Subhadra's hand in marriage to Duryodhana. But when he saw that Subhadra's heart was set on Arjuna, he gave up the idea. Subhadra and Arjuna were married and had a brave son named Abhimanyu. When he was in the womb of his mother, Abhimanyu learnt a lot of war strategies from his father, Arjuna. In fact, he learnt about the Chakravyuha also when he was in his mother's womb. Arjuna was enthusiastically describing the Chakravyuha to Subhadra, who was least interested in such things. At one point, she went to sleep, but the baby in her womb kept hearing attentively. When Arjuna saw Subhadra fast asleep, he stopped the narration abruptly, and thus Abhimanyu only heard about how to enter the Chakravyuha and not the exit strategy.

Subhadra's son Abhimanyu was married to Uttara, the princess of the Virata kingdom, and they had the most illustrious Parikshit as their son. Thus, Subhadra was the grandmother of Parikshit.

Sulochana
From Ramayana

Sulochana was born under unique circumstances. One day, Parvati was helping Shiva to dress up. She handed him his tiger skin and his rudraksh mala. She coiled the snake Vasuki around Shiva's wrist a bit too tight. Vasuki winced in pain and two teardrops fell on the ground. The teardrops turned into two girls, Sunaina and Sulochana. An argument ensued between Vasuki and Parvati over who was the parent of the girls. Both Vasuki and Parvati wanted ownership over the girls.

Since the tears fell from the snake's eyes, the snake felt the daughters belonged to him. Parvati claimed it was her act of coiling the snake too tight that caused the birth of the girls, and so she was the rightful mother. Unable to solve the dilemma, they asked Shiva to intervene. Shiva advised them to take one child each. Sunaina was given to Parvati and Sulochana to the Nagas. Sunaina was eventually married to King Janaka and was Sita's mother. Sulochana was taken by the Nagas, raised as the daughter of Sheshanag and later married to Meghnad, Ravana's elder son.

In the war between Rama and Ravana, Meghnad was killed by Lakshman. When Sulochana heard of his death, Ravana directed her to claim his head from Rama. Unafraid, Sulochana entered the enemy camp and was respectfully received by Rama. She collected her husband's head from Rama and, on the shores of the ocean, sat on the funeral pyre and gave up her life. Sulochana proved that she was a brave and chaste woman who did not shy from fulfilling her duties.

Sumitra
From Ramayana

Sumitra was the princess of Kashi, King Dasharatha's second queen, and the mother of Lakshmana and Shatrughna. She was considered the wisest of the three queens. King Dasharatha once performed a yajna to beget children. From the fire sacrifice, Dasharatha received nectar that he divided into four parts to distribute among his three queens. He gave Sumitra two portions as he respected her attitude of selfless service. Sumitra passed on her attitude of service to her twins, Lakshmana and Shatrughna. Lakshmana's life mission was to serve Shri Rama, whereas Shatrughna served Bharata.

When Lakshmana went to Sumitra to seek permission to go to the forest with Rama, he was afraid that she would try to stop him. Instead, she advised him that from now on, his father was not Dasharatha, but his elder brother Rama. She was not his mother, Sita was. Last, the palace of Ayodhya was not his home, the forest was his home now. His life was to serve Rama and Sita.

Before leaving Ayodhya, Rama did not seek permission from Sumitra. That never bothered her, as she had experienced the love and respect of Rama her whole life. From Sumitra, we learn that where there is love, there is trust. The name Sumitra means 'one who is a good friend', and throughout the Ramayana that remains Sumitra's character- a well-wishing friend to everyone.

Suniti

From Shrimad Bhagavatam

Suniti was one of the two wives of King Uttanapada, the descendent of Manu and a king in the Solar dynasty. Though Suniti was beautiful and intelligent, King Uttanapada favoured his other wife Suruchi, and neglected her. Suniti and her son Dhruva had to tolerate the atrocities and ill words of Suruchi. Suniti raised her son Dhruva with a lot of love and care. But Dhruva always hankered for the love of his father. Whenever he saw his stepbrother Uttama sitting on his father's lap, he felt neglected. One day, when his stepbrother was absent, he tried to sit on his father's lap along with Uttama. Unfortunately, Suruchi arrived just then. She was furious at the five-year-old Dhruva and chastised him harshly. She told him that if he wanted to sit on his father's lap, he would have to die and take birth again from her womb. For that, she advised him to pray to Lord Narayan to help fulfil his desire.

Little Dhruva was devastated by the treatment of his stepmother. He ran to his mother Suniti and narrated to her the entire story, shedding torrents of tears. Suniti understood his predicament and guided her son with wise words. Suniti asked Dhruva to focus on and take shelter of Lord Narayan. Dhruva followed his mother's advice and became the most celebrated devotee of Lord Narayan for all time to come. He eventually got the love of his father that he so dearly craved.

Surasa

From Ramayana, Matsya Purana

Surasa was the mother of the Nagas (serpents). She lived in the ocean and was sent by the gods to test Hanuman on his journey to Lanka to rescue Sita from the clutches of Ravana.

When Hanuman was flying over the ocean, Surasa blocked his path. She did not allow him to cross. Surasa was blessed with a boon from Lord Brahma that she could eat any one who flew over the ocean. Hanuman was in a hurry to reach Lanka. He did not have time to argue with her, but she would not let him go. She glared at him with her reddish-brown eyes.

Suddenly, Hanuman expanded and became ten times her size. His sudden resizing clearly shocked Surasa. Her gaping mouth became wider until it was almost twenty times his size. Hanuman then outmatched her by expanding thirty times more than Surasa. She went a notch higher, and her mouth was now forty times as wide. Hanuman outdid her again. Her exceedingly wide mouth and head were now kissing the clouds.

Hanuman then unexpectedly shrunk himself to the size of a thumb. He zoomed into the Nagas! "I have fulfilled Brahma's boon without compromising my mission. I have entered your mouth and also exited it. Kindly allow me to proceed on this extremely important mission to Maa Sita." With folded hands, Hanuman begged her for permission to continue.

Surasa's heart melted. Seeing his humility, she could no longer remain fierce. She told him she was sent by the gods to test him and had no intention of harming him. She then blessed him and prayed for the success of his mission like a mother.

Susheela

From Srimad Bhagavatam

Susheela was the wife of Sudama, a very poor Brahmin. Sudama and Krishna had studied in the same Gurukul of Sandipani Muni and had become the best of friends. After leaving the Gurukul, Krishna became the King of Dwarka, and Sudama lived in a small village with his wife and children. They even lacked basic needs like food and shelter but they never complained nor tried to become rich through dishonest means.

Gradually, the size of their family grew and they had nothing to feed their children. For the sake of her young ones, a desperate Susheela requested her husband to seek help from his childhood friend, Lord Krishna, who was the King of Dwarka.

Sudama finally agreed on the condition that he would not ask him for anything himself. He would accept whatever Krishna would give him.

Wanting to meet his old friend, Sudama was eager to carry some gift for Krishna. Susheela went door-to-door begging and thus collected four fistfuls of chipped rice from four houses. She packed the stale, chipped rice in a pouch and handed it over to Sudama as a gift for Krishna. When Sudama reached Dwarka, Krishna treated Sudama with great respect and love. Sudama was embarrassed to give him the chipped rice. But Krishna knew all and requested Sudama to give him the chipped rice which Sushila had sent for him. Krishna ate that rice with relish.

Sudama basked in his love without asking for anything, and Krishna offered nothing himself. When Sudama reached home, his small hut had transformed into a massive palace and his wife, and the children were dressed in the most opulent manner. They lived in gratitude and devotion to Krishna for the rest of their lives.

Swayamprabha
From Ramayana

Swayamprabha was the maid of an apsara named Hema who came from the heavens and married Mayasura, the asura master architect. Mayasura became world famous for his architectural designs. He offered his wife a mystical city that was the epitome of his creation and he named it Hemapura. However, he did not live long and was killed by Indra. Highly disappointed by the death of her husband, Hema apsara left for her heavenly home, handing over the charge of the mystical city to Swayamprabha. Swayamprabha lost all interest in worldly enjoyment and embraced a life of austerities and yogic practices. She lived in a mystical cave in the city.

When the Vanaras were searching for Mother Sita in the southern direction, they stumbled upon this dark cavity, which was the opening to a mystical cave. When they entered the cave, it was so huge and complicated that they lost their path and got stuck in the middle of the cave, not knowing their way out. That is when they came across the effulgent looking Swayamprabha. Seeing that they were famished, she first fed them lavishly. The monkeys were grateful for her hospitality. Then the monkeys asked her for directions to exit the cave. She instructed them to close their eyes and used her yogic powers to transport them mystically outside the cave. The cave opened up towards the Southern Ocean and the monkeys were on the right path again.

Tara
From Ramayana

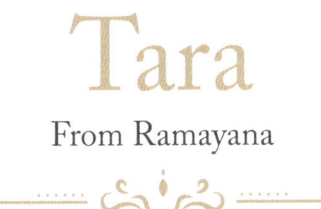

Tara was the queen of Kishkindha, the land of the Vanaras. In some versions, she was said to be the daughter of Brihaspati, the guru of gods. In others, she was the daughter of the vanara physician Sushena. She was the wife of Vali and the mother of Angad, the prince of the land. When Sugriva came to challenge his brother Vali for a fight, Tara warned Vali not to venture out, as she suspected that the normally weak Sugriva was showing unprecedented over-confidence and there was definitely someone powerful backing him. Vali, in his pride, ignored Tara's advice and went outside. Eventually, Lord Rama killed Vali with a single arrow.

After Vali's death, Tara had a deep conversation with Rama that showed her intelligence and devotion. Although Tara lamented her husband's death, she acknowledged Rama as the Supreme Lord. She then became queen of Sugriva, as per the norms of that time. After Sugriva became the king of Kishkindha, he immersed in indulgences and totally forgot his promise to Rama. Having waited sufficiently, Rama sent Lakshmana to remind Sugriva of his promise. Lakshmana barged into Kishkindha and was ready to destroy the city. However, Tara, acting as the chief diplomat of Sugriva's court, pacified Lakshmana, causing the reconciliation between Rama and Sugriva.

Because of her intelligence, courage and devotion, she was one of the most revered women in the Ramayana.

The Wives of Kaliya
From Srimad Bhagavatam

Nagapatnis were the wives of Kaliya, the thousand-headed snake that took over a lake connected to the Yamuna River in Vrindavan. They were great devotees of Lord Krishna. Unlike Kaliya, the Nagapatnis loved Krishna with all their heart and believed that their husband would one day change. Kaliya, who was hiding from Garuda, chose to reside in Vrindavan as it was the only place where Garuda could not hunt him without meeting his own death. The Nagapatnis were not happy with their husband's choice to stay in Vrindavan, knowing that their beloved Krishna lives there. They knew that wherever their husband went, destruction and suffering followed.

Soon after Kaliya entered the waters of Yamuna in Vrindavan, the lake became poisonous. One day, Krishna visited the lake with his friends and cows. His friends jumped into the lake in joy and instantly died. Krishna revived the boys and jumped into the lake himself. Krishna defeated the wicked serpent by dancing on his head. He almost killed the serpent when his wives, the Nagapatanis appeared with folded hands, begging him to spare the life of their husband. Krishna pardoned the serpent by performing a last dance on his head.

After the dance, Krishna asked Kaliya to leave the waters of Yamuna and return to Ramanaka Island. He also ensured him that he would no longer be hunted by Garuda. Kaliya was saved by the devotion and purity of his wives. He was asked to follow the examples of his wives and let go of his arrogance and ego.

Tilottama
From Mahabharata

Once, Brahma granted a boon to the demon brothers, Nanda and Upananda, that no one could kill them except themselves. The brothers turned absolutely berserk and plundered the entire Universe. Brahma had to find a way to undo the horrendous boon he had given them.

Brahma approached Vishwakarma with his game plan. Vishwakarma, the celestial architect, selected the best of precious gems and beautiful elements from all over the Universe and shaped a beautiful apsara out of them. He named her Tilotamma, one who radiates beauty.

Tilotamma found the demonic brothers revelling along a river bank. Her breathtaking looks caught Nanda's and Upananda's eyes. They had never seen anyone so beautiful. Unable to take their eyes off her, both felt an intense desire to ask for her hand in marriage.

Without wasting a moment, both of them rushed to Tilotamma. Nanda grabbed her left hand and Upananda, her right. Each pulled her towards themselves. Overcome by desire, their brotherly love vanished.

Unable to bear the thought of losing her, they attacked each other. The madness to marry her had taken away their common sense. They had forgotten Brahma's boon. They charged at each other with a club in their hands with the only intention of killing the other. Striking hard on the head, and roaring with utmost ferocity, the two clubbed each other to death.

All the devatas thanked and congratulated Tilottama for her superb performance. Brahma even granted her a boon that no one could look at her for more than a few moments.

Trijata
From Ramayana

Trijata was one of the very special Rakshasis from Lanka. She was the daughter of Vibhishan and the favourite niece of Ravana. Ravana loved her so much that he gave her the charge of his favourite garden, Ashoka Vatika. She was clairvoyant and could perceive things that ordinarily could not be perceived by others.

In fact, she dreamt of a monkey roaming around in Ashok Vatika and speaking with Sita. She also saw the golden city of Lanka in flames. A vanara was prancing around everywhere, smiling as the city burned. When Hanuman heard Trijata's dream, he realised that saints could exist in Lanka as well. He was thrilled to see such divinity in a place like Lanka.

Everything she dreamt turned out to be true. She protected Sita from the torture of other demonesses by warning them not to bother her, as she was a very divine being. In another dream, she saw Rama wearing a beautiful white garland approaching Lanka in flying chariot that was drawn by a thousand white swans, and carrying away Sita. Throughout Sita's stay in Lanka, Trijata provided her great moral support and encouragement.

During the war, Ravana told Trijata to take Sita to see the dead Rama and Lakshmana as proof that they were actually dead. Trijata obeyed Ravana and took Sita over the battlefield in the Pushpaka Vimana. As soon as they saw the fallen brothers, Sita burst out in tears, thinking that they were indeed dead. However, Trijata convinced Sita that they were actually not dead and this was just an illusion created by Ravana to make her miserable. Trijata was a kind and saintly demoness who represents the ray of hope in the greatest hour of darkness.

Tulasi

From Devi Bhagavat Purana

Tulasi is the consort of Lord Krishna and the incarnation of Goddess Mahalakshmi herself. Mahalakshmi entered the womb of Queen Madhavi and was born after a hundred years. Her name means, 'one who is matchless' or 'incomparable'. From the very beginning, Tulasi worshipped Bhagavan Vishnu and desired him as her husband. When her desire intensified, she left for Badrikashram in the Himalayas. She lived for twenty-four thousand years surviving on fruits and water, the next thirty thousand years on leaves, then forty thousand years on air and another ten thousand years without eating or drinking anything. Brahma appeared before her to inquire why she was indulging in such intense penance. On learning of her desire, he informed her that she would surely marry Bhagavan Vishnu, one day.

When the pious Tulasi left Earth, a part of her body remained behind as the holy plant Tulasi. Tulasi plant is very dear to Vishnu, and no worship is complete without the offering of Tulasi. Tulasi's life of purity and love for Vishnu is the most powerful example of purposeful living.

Lord Krishna lives with Tulasi, and singing glories of Tulasi please him. Association with Tulasi in any way is purifying for the soul. Thus, the Vaishnavas wear Tulasi beads around their necks, give Tulasi as gifts and use Tulasi incense.

Ubhaya Bharataai

From Folklore

Ubhaya Bharataai lived in Mithila, the kingdom of King Janak and Sita. Her husband, Mandana Mishra, and she were highly learned in Vedic literature. Their Vedic lifestyle included not only studying the scriptures but applying it daily in their lives by doing yagyas and rituals to please the ancestors, sages and gods. They were in union with nature. They would undertake deep introspection to find the nature of the soul. Even the parrots outside their house could be heard discussing concepts from the Vedas.

Once, the well-known scholar Adi Shankaracharya came to visit this special couple. He began a discussion with Mandana Mishra which soon turned into a debate. Every debate needs a neutral moderator, so they elected Ubhaya Bharataai to moderate. Both were brilliant and learned, which made her job tough; and tougher because one of them was her husband. Mandana, however, was agitated with Shankaracharya's arguments, because of which the garland around his neck began to wither. Although he was on an equal footing with his opponent in terms of knowledge, he could not keep his cool. Considering this, Ubhaya Bharataai declared Shankaracharya the winner. Her righteousness, sense of fairness and impartiality impressed even Shankaracharya.

Ulupi
From Mahabharata

Ulupi was the daughter of the king of the Nagas, Kaurava. The Naga family lived at the bottom of the Bhagirathi River. Ulupi would often come out of her watery domain and visit a temple of Lord Shiva situated on the bank of the river. One day, when she was exiting from the temple, her eyes fell on Arjuna, who visited the riverside frequently. He was sitting in a lotus posture in intense meditation. The moment her eyes fell on him, she instantly fell in love. She kept staring at him for a long period. Finally, she decided to kidnap him.

When Arjuna completed his meditation and went to have a bath in the river, he suddenly felt drowsy and collapsed. Ulupi rushed to hold him and carried him along with her to the Nagaloka, situated at the river bed. She arranged a comfortable bed for him to rest on. When Arjuna woke up, he was shocked to see himself inside the river, sleeping on a celestial bed. Staring at him was the most gorgeous woman who seemed to be out of the world.

Ulupi expressed her love, and they spent a few days together. Eventually, Ulupi gave birth to Arjuna's son named Iravan. When Arjuna left, Ulupi wished to stay back in her Naga abode with her son. Later, in the Mahabharata war, Ulupi sent her son to assist Arjuna in the war. Iravan was killed in the battle by Alambush, the demon who fought for the Kauravas.

Uma Haimavati
From Kenopanishad

Uma Haimavati the wife of Rudra is a goddess higher than Agni, Vayu and Indra.

Once, after defeating the asuras in battle, the devas became proud and arrogant of their strength. Seeing this inflated ego, Rudra decided to bring the devas back to their senses.

Rudra appeared before the devas as a yaksha. The devas could not recognise him. So Indra sent Agni to find out his identity. A puffed up Agni introduced himself as the god of fire who could burn the whole Universe down if he so desired. The amused yaksha stretched out his hand, holding a blade of hay.

"Can you burn this?" he asked.

Agni took a deep breath and blew on the blade. The hay remained untouched. Unable to face the humiliation, Agni left. Indra then sent Vayu to find out the yaksha's identity. Vayu haughtily declared that he ruled the winds and he could create a cyclone. The yaksha handed him the same blade of hay and asked him to blow it away. Vayu tried, but the piece of hay did not move an inch.

A bewildered Indra himself paid a visit to the yaksha. But instead of the yaksha, there stood before him the universal mother, Uma Haimavati. She told him that the powers that the gods possessed came from the Supreme Being, and there was no reason for them to be arrogant. She said that it was her, Uma, the Shakti who controlled the Universe as the divine mother, not the gods. Indra paid his respect to the divine mother and thanked her for showing him the right path.

Urmila

From Ramayana

Like her elder sister Sita, Urmila faced many challenging situations in life and made great sacrifices. Urmila's husband Lakshmana wanted to leave with Rama for exile in order to serve Rama and Sita. That meant a fourteen year-long separation from her husband. Lakshmana was apprehensive about how Urmila would react to it. He wondered if Urmila would try to stop him from going. To his surprise, Urmila understood his sentiments and respected his desire to serve Rama. She did not wish to be an obstacle in Lakshmana's life.

While Sita had her husband by her side during exile, at least for some time, Urmila lived without her husband and served her mothers-in-law in Ayodhya. She never complained about her situation even once and fulfilled all her duties with utmost sincerity.

While in exile, Lakshmana had taken a vow to forsake sleep for fourteen years to better serve and protect Rama and Sita. Nidra Devi, the goddess of sleep, herself came to ask Lakshmana to sleep and accept her service, but Lakshmana refused. Instead, he sent her to Urmila so Nidra Devi could serve her.

Nidra Devi left for Ayodhya. Urmila accepted her request, as she did not want Lakshmana to worry about her and get distracted from his duties. She slept for the next fourteen years during the day on behalf of Lakshmana and for herself at night. Although Lakshmana and Urmila were far away from each other, their hearts always remained with each other.

Usha

From Shrimad Bhagavatam

Usha was the daughter of Banasura, the most powerful Asura King of Sonitpur. Banasura was one of the greatest devotees of Lord Shiva. Lord Shiva had blessed him with a thousand arms. Usha herself was a great devotee of Lord Shiva and his wife Parvati. She once prayed to Parvati and when Parvati appeared, Usha asked her who would be her future husband. Parvati answered that Usha would have a dream in the month of Baisakh in which she would see her future husband.

Exactly as predicted, Usha saw a handsome young prince in her dream and it was love at first sight. When she woke up the next day, her friend Chitralekha helped her illustrate the prince. When they realised it was Anirudha, the prince of Dwarka, son of Pradyumna and the grandson of Lord Krishna, they were dumbstruck. The next night, Chitralekha used her mystical powers and air lifted Anirudha along with his bed and brought him to Usha. Anirudha and Usha instantly liked each other.

When Krishna realised his grandson was kidnapped, he attacked Banasura's kingdom. Banasura had no clue why he was being attacked and invoked Lord Shiva's presence. The fight between Shiva and Krishna ended with Shiva falling unconscious. Krishna attacked Banasura and just when he was about to kill him, Lord Shiva woke up and requested Krishna to spare his disciple's life. Krishna forgave Banasura on the condition that the marriage takes place as per the wishes of Uma and Aniruddha. Usha and Aniruddha got married and had a son named Vajra.

Uttara
From Mahabharata

Uttara was the daughter of King Virata, who gave shelter to the Pandavas while they were incognito for a year. Uttar Kumar was her brother. While the Pandavas lived there, they served the King of Virata in many roles. Arjuna was disguised as Brihannala, an eunuch. He taught Uttara singing and dancing skills. Once the King of Virata got to know that Brihannala is actually the great Pandava Arjuna, he offered his daughter Uttara in marriage to Arjuna. But Arjuna denied the proposal, stating that he had always looked upon her as a student, like his daughter, and thus could not think of her in this way. But he proposed that his son, Abhimanyu, would be a good match for Uttara. So Uttara was married to Abhimanyu. Unfortunately, she soon became a widow. Abhimanyu was killed on the battlefield of Kurukshetra.

When Abhimanyu died, Uttara was pregnant. After the war got over, Ashwatthama, the son of Dronacharya, was frustrated due to all his losses and decided to do one last thing to avenge it all. He hurled the Brahmastra at the womb of Uttara in an attempt to destroy the yet to be born child right in the womb of his mother. Krishna entered the womb of Uttara and revived the dead child. The revived child of Uttara was Parikshit, who became a great king and successor to the kingdom of the Pandavas. Eventually, Parikshit heard the Shrimad Bhagavatam from Sukhdev Goswami. He then narrated the same Bhagavatam to his mother, Uttara, just before departing from this world.

Urvashi

From Mahabharata

Urvashi was a beautiful apsara created by Sage Naranarayan. She then went to live in the heavenly kingdom, in the court of King Indra.

Urvashi means one who can conquer hearts. She was eternally beautiful and so mesmerising that many men wanted to win her heart. But she lost her heart to a king on Earth called King Pururavas, an ancestor of the Pandavas. Urvashi married him and had a wonderful life on Earth till Indra asked her to come back to heaven.

Once, Indra invited Arjuna to heaven to give him the celestial weapons. Together, they watched the heavenly apsaras dance in the court. Indra noticed Arjuna looking at Urvashi repeatedly. The reason Arjuna was staring at her was because he knew that his ancestor had been married to her. Time in heaven differs from time on Earth and apsaras never age. Arjuna wanted to have a good look at one of his great-great-great-grandmothers. But Indra misunderstood him. He thought Arjuna was staring at her because he was attracted to her.

After the evening dance performance, he asked Urvashi to meet Arjuna. Urvashi, too, liked the handsome and well-built Arjuna.

She happily went to meet Arjuna, but she got the shock of her life at what he told her. When she proposed to him, he said Urvashi was a mother figure for him, so how could he accept a proposal from a mother? Apsara felt insulted by Arjuna's refusal. She did not feel old enough to be his mother. She cursed Arjuna that he would become a eunuch. This curse actually helped Arjuna disguise himself later, during his exile.

Vedavati

From Ramayana

Vedavati was born to a sage named Kushadhwaja. Her birth itself was most auspicious as she appeared amid the chanting of Vedic mantras. As she was born during the chanting of Vedas, she was called Vedavati. Right from her birth, she was a great devotee of Lord Vishnu. As she grew up, she became adamant that she would only marry Vishnu and no mortal man of this world. She performed great tapasya in order to fulfil her desire. After a long period of tapasya, she heard a celestial voice declaring that in her next life, she would have Lord Vishnu as her husband.

During this time, Ravana, the king of Lanka, was hovering around the mountain on which Vedavati was performing her austerities. The moment he spotted her divine beauty seated on the mountaintop with eyes closed in deep meditation, Ravana fell in love with her. He wanted to marry her. He jumped off his chariot, and proposed to the shocked Vedavati. When she refused, Ravana lost his patience and pulled her by her hair. Using her yogic powers, she chopped off the section of her hair that he held, and self-immolated herself, cursing him that she would return to be the cause of his death.

When Rama left to bring the golden deer to Sita, he handed Sita to Agni, the fire god, for her protection. Agni sent the Maya Sita, who was actually Vedavati, to replace the real Sita. Ravana kidnapped Vedavati instead of Sita. Vedavati posed as the wife of Rama for those ten months in Lanka and actually became the cause of Ravana's death. Eventually, when Ravana was killed, the Agni Pareeksha or test by fire was conducted in which Vedavati returned to Agni and the real Sita was reunited with Rama.

Vidula

From Mahabharata

Vidula was a queen and a brave mother who inspired her son, Sanjaya, to beat all odds and defeat his enemies in battle.

Vidula had lost her husband and her son, Sanjaya, had been crowned king. He was inexperienced, which made him an easy target for the neighbouring kings. The king of Sindhu defeated Sanjaya easily in war, as he lacked experience and confidence. When Sanjaya returned to his palace after the defeat, he was morose and unmotivated. When Vidula saw his condition, she had a dialogue with him. She said, "For a Kshatriya, it is better to show valour for a day and die, rather than be a coward and stay alive."

When Sanjaya asked her why she wanted to see him dead or defeated, she gave him a fitting reply.

"It is better to have dependents rather than depend on others."

She continued to inspire him with stories of heroism and persistence. Vidula reminded him of the glories of his ancestors. She also gave him war strategies to fight the king of Sindhu. The Sindhu king had many enemies who would join hands with Sanjaya. Some kings would join him for wealth and some kings were friends waiting to offer their help. Pooling in all these resources, he could easily attain success. The secret of success, she said, was in acting and not in avoiding. With her words, she inspired her son, who eventually defeated the king of Sindhu.

Vinata

From Ramayana

Vinata and Kadru were sisters, both married to Sage Kashyap. Vinata's woes began when the powerful sage granted them a boon. Kadru asked for a thousand brave sons as her boon but Vinata got bitten by the bug of jealousy and asked for sons who were better than Kadru's sons. After his wives became pregnant, Sage Kashyap left for his penance in the forest. So Kadru gave birth to a thousand snakes and Vinata laid two eggs.

Vinata waited for five hundred long years for the eggs to hatch, but nothing happened. Overcome by impatience, she broke open one egg. The bird inside was only half-formed and came out handicapped. Angry with his mother, he cursed her that she would spend five hundred years as a slave of Kadru and the curse would end with the birth of his brother from the second egg.

Time went by and Vinata was tricked by Kadru into becoming her slave. When Garuda was born five hundred years later, he too inherited the slavery. Garuda was brighter than fire and extremely powerful. He shone so brightly that his presence was blinding. The demigods asked him to reduce his effulgence so they could see properly. Despite his strength and aura, he was a slave to Kadru, which made him extremely angry. He asked Kadru and her sons about the price of releasing his mother. They asked him to get them the immortal nectar from heaven. It was a laborious task, but with his parent's blessings, he accomplished the task and released his mother Vinata from bondage.

Vishnupriya
From Caitanya Caritamrita

Vishnupriya was the incarnation of Bhumidevi and the eternal consort of the Supreme Lord. She was born to the great Brahmin Sanatana Mishra in Navadvipa. Right from her early childhood, she worshipped Mother Ganga with great devotion and served the elders of the village with all her respect and devotion. When Sachi Mata, the mother of Lord Chaitanya, observed her wonderful nature, she felt that Vishnupriya would be the ideal match for her son Nimai, who eventually came to be known as Chaitanya Mahaprabhu. Both the families immediately agreed, and the marriage took place with great pomp and enthusiasm.

Nimai and Vishnupriya understood each other perfectly and would serve everyone who came to their house with great love. Though they had servants, Vishnupriya preferred to do everything herself as she considered service as a privilege and not a burden. She took excellent care of Sachi Mata, who was getting old.

In order to preach the message of spirituality, Nimai decided to take sanyas. Vishnupriya was heartbroken but lived the rest of her life in separation from Lord Chaitanya, who travelled around the country, transforming the lives of millions of souls.

Vishnupriya would chant the holy names of God on her beads and after each round, she would keep one grain of rice aside. Whatever grains she collected by chanting all day, she would cook it, offer it to the deity of her husband, and eat that for the day. Such was her austerity. Her life was the perfect example of devotion, sacrifice and service to the Supreme Lord.

Vrushali
From Mahabharata

Vrushali was the sister of Satyasena, the chariot driver of Duryodhana. Vrushali's family hailed from Prayag, the confluence of Rivers Ganga, Yamuna and Saraswati. Satysena, Vrushali and Karna were childhood friends. Both Karna and Vrushali's fathers agreed to get Karna and Vrushali married. Vrushali and Karna had ten sons: Vrishasena, Sudama, Vrishaketu, Chitrasena, Satyasena, Sushena, Shatrunjaya, Dvipata, Banasena and Prasena.

Eight of her sons took part in the Kurukshetra war of the Mahabharata. Arjuna killed Shatrunjaya, Vrishasena, and Dvipata. Bhima killed Banasena. Chitrasena, Satyasena and Sushena were killed by Nakula. Vrishaketu was the only survivor of Vrushali's sons. Vrishaketu had the patronage of Arjuna even before Karna's death. He also took part in the battles which Arjuna fought during the Ashwamedha Yagya.

After Karna's death, Vrushali was heartbroken and gave up her life by practising sati. Duryodhana appreciated Vrushali as an extraordinary woman. Gandhari too praised Vrushali as a brave woman. Even though there is not much written about Vrushali in the Mahabharata, she's been the subject of many books and novels.

Yamuna

From Srimad Bhagavatam

Yamuna was the daughter of Surya, the sun god, and his wife Sandhya, a cloud goddess. She is also known as Yami and Suryatanaya (the daughter of Surya). Yama was the god of death and Yami was his twin sister. Her mother Sandhya could not tolerate the radiance of their father and left home. She went to a forest in the guise of a mare to meditate and sent her shadow Chhaya (her lookalike) to take care of her children.

Chhaya started neglecting Yama and Yamuna. Chhaya punished them without reason and had no affection for them. Unable to take this cruel treatment, Yama stomped on Chhaya's foot one day. A curse shot out of her mouth. Since he had caused pain to her foot, she cursed Yama that he would lose his foot.

Yamuna heard this awful curse and was terrified. She did not want her brother to lose a foot. She immediately went to Earth to pray for the curse to be revoked. The distraught Yamuna wept and wept and her tears became the river Yamuna.

Yamuna is considered as sacred as the River Ganga. Bathing in her waters or drinking her water frees one from all sins. The confluence of Yamuna, Ganga and Saraswati called Triveni Sangam, is the holiest of all places. Sri Krishna spent his youth on the banks of the Yamuna. She is also known as Kalindi because her waters are blackish because she is the sister of Yama, the god of darkness.

Yashoda

From Srimad Bhagavatam

Yashoda is famously remembered as the foster mother of Krishna. She was the wife of Gokul's chieftain Nanda. There are many adorable stories of Krishna and Yashoda. One such story is that on Diwali, when Krishna was a toddler, Yashoda got up very early to cook various special sweets for her little son. While she was busy cooking, little Krishna woke up. He crawled out of bed, looking for her. When he found her churning butter, he was very upset that she chose to do this chore instead of cuddling him. He stopped her churning and caught her saree to demand her attention.

Yashoda immediately picked him up and nourished him with her milk. As she continued to churn the butter simultaneously, the milk on the stove started boiling over. She immediately left Krishna on the floor to attend to the milk. The abandonment by his mother during his greatest bliss triggered Krishna's anger. He created havoc in the storehouse by throwing things all over and messing up the whole place. A few minutes later, when Yashoda returned, she decided to punish the little culprit, who had now run away with the pot of butter. She found him in the courtyard, feeding the butter that she had so painstakingly churned, to a band of monkeys. She caught him and attempted to tie him to a grinding stone. No matter how much she tried, the rope was two fingers too short. After hours of trying, Krishna felt sorry for his poor mother and allowed himself to be tied up.

What great yogis could not achieve by meditating for millions of years, a simple mother in Vrindavan achieved with her love. Krishna also showed Yashoda his Divine Form.